OPPOSING
VIEWPOINTS®
SERIES

Iran

Other Books of Related Interest:

Opposing Viewpoints Series

Iraq

Israel

Human Rights

The Middle East

National Security

Terrorism

Weapons of Mass Destruction

Current Controversies Series

America's Battle Against Terrorism

Homeland Security

Interventionism

The Middle East

Violence Against Women

Weapons of Mass Destruction

At Issue Series

Are Efforts to Reduce Terrorism Successful?

Biological and Chemical Weapons

Can Democracy Succeed in the Middle East?

Do Nuclear Weapons Pose a Serious Threat?

Homeland Security

Is Iran a Threat to Global Security?

National Security

Nuclear Security

U.S. Policy Toward Rogue Nations

What Are the Most Serious Threats to National Security?

"Congress shall make no law . . . abridging the freedom of speech, or of the press."

First Amendment to the U.S. Constitution

The basic foundation of our democracy is the First Amendment guarantee of freedom of expression. The Opposing Viewpoints Series is dedicated to the concept of this basic freedom and the idea that it is more important to practice it than to enshrine it.

Iran

Laura K. Egendorf, Book Editor

GREENHAVEN PRESS

An imprint of Thomson Gale, a part of The Thomson Corporation

Detroit • New York • San Francisco • New Haven, Conn. • Waterville, Maine • London

Christine Nasso, *Publisher*
Elizabeth Des Chenes, *Managing Editor*

© 2006 Thomson Gale, a part of The Thomson Corporation.

Thomson and Star logo are trademarks and Gale and Greenhaven Press are registered trademarks used herein under license.

For more information, contact:
Greenhaven Press
27500 Drake Rd.
Farmington Hills, MI 48331-3535
Or you can visit our Internet site at http://www.gale.com

LIBRARY OF CONGRESS CATALOGING-IN-PUBLICATION DATA

Iran / Laura K. Egendorf, book editor.
    p. cm. -- (Opposing viewpoints)
    Includes bibliographical references and index.
    ISBN-13: 978-0-7377-3417-1 (harcover lib. : alk. paper)
    ISBN-10: 0-7377-3417-5 (hardcover lib. : alk. paper)
    ISBN-13: 978-0-7377-3418-8 (pbk. : alk. paper)
    ISBN-10: 0-7377-3418-3 (pbk. : alk. paper)
    1. Iran--Politics and government--1997– 2. Iran--Foreign relations --1997–
    I. Egendorf, Laura K., 1973–
    DS318.9.I725 2007
    955.05'44--dc22
                                                        2006016934

Printed in the United States of America
10 9 8 7 6 5 4 3 2 1

Contents

Why Consider Opposing Viewpoints?

> *"The only way in which a human being can make some approach to knowing the whole of a subject is by hearing what can be said about it by persons of every variety of opinion and studying all modes in which it can be looked at by every character of mind. No wise man ever acquired his wisdom in any mode but this."*
>
> *John Stuart Mill*

In our media-intensive culture it is not difficult to find differing opinions. Thousands of newspapers and magazines and dozens of radio and television talk shows resound with differing points of view. The difficulty lies in deciding which opinion to agree with and which "experts" seem the most credible. The more inundated we become with differing opinions and claims, the more essential it is to hone critical reading and thinking skills to evaluate these ideas. Opposing Viewpoints books address this problem directly by presenting stimulating debates that can be used to enhance and teach these skills. The varied opinions contained in each book examine many different aspects of a single issue. While examining these conveniently edited opposing views, readers can develop critical thinking skills such as the ability to compare and contrast authors' credibility, facts, argumentation styles, use of persuasive techniques, and other stylistic tools. In short, the Opposing Viewpoints Series is an ideal way to attain the higher-level thinking and reading skills so essential in a culture of diverse and contradictory opinions.

In addition to providing a tool for critical thinking, Opposing Viewpoints books challenge readers to question their own strongly held opinions and assumptions. Most people form their opinions on the basis of upbringing, peer pressure, and personal, cultural, or professional bias. By reading carefully balanced opposing views, readers must directly confront new ideas as well as the opinions of those with whom they disagree. This is not to simplistically argue that everyone who reads opposing views will—or should—change his or her opinion. Instead, the series enhances readers' understanding of their own views by encouraging confrontation with opposing ideas. Careful examination of others' views can lead to the readers' understanding of the logical inconsistencies in their own opinions, perspective on why they hold an opinion, and the consideration of the possibility that their opinion requires further evaluation.

Evaluating Other Opinions

To ensure that this type of examination occurs, Opposing Viewpoints books present all types of opinions. Prominent spokespeople on different sides of each issue as well as well-known professionals from many disciplines challenge the reader. An additional goal of the series is to provide a forum for other, less known, or even unpopular viewpoints. The opinion of an ordinary person who has had to make the decision to cut off life support from a terminally ill relative, for example, may be just as valuable and provide just as much insight as a medical ethicist's professional opinion. The editors have two additional purposes in including these less known views. One, the editors encourage readers to respect others' opinions—even when not enhanced by professional credibility. It is only by reading or listening to and objectively evaluating others' ideas that one can determine whether they are worthy of consideration. Two, the inclusion of such viewpoints encourages the important critical thinking skill of objectively evaluating an author's credentials and bias. This evaluation will illuminate an author's reasons for taking a particular stance on an issue and will aid in readers' evaluation of the author's ideas.

It is our hope that these books will give readers a deeper understanding of the issues debated and an appreciation of the complexity of even seemingly simple issues when good and honest people disagree. This awareness is particularly important in a democratic society such as ours in which people enter into public debate to determine the common good. Those with whom one disagrees should not be regarded as enemies but rather as people whose views deserve careful examination and may shed light on one's own.

Thomas Jefferson once said that "difference of opinion leads to inquiry, and inquiry to truth." Jefferson, a broadly educated man, argued that "if a nation expects to be ignorant and free . . . it expects what never was and never will be." As individuals and as a nation, it is imperative that we consider the opinions of others and examine them with skill and discernment. The Opposing Viewpoints Series is intended to help readers achieve this goal.

David L. Bender and Bruno Leone,
Founders

Introduction

"Iranians are ethnically Persian—not Ar-abs. The people of Iran hearken back to an imperial Persian heritage. Their sense of Persian history and culture is deep and defines them uniquely from their Arab neighbors."

—Edward Gnehm,
professor of international affairs

"For 2,000 years . . . Iran has been the intellectual heart of the Middle East, but as a part of the Middle East with 250 million Arabs. . . . We have to acknowl-edge the commonality of our history."

—Loay Abdelkarim,
journalist

Iran is a nation of approximately 68 million people, 97 per-cent of whom practice Islam. It is located in the Middle East, but Iran is not an Arab country. While Iran shares the same religion and region as its Arab neighbors, it is a country whose unique Persian history and identity remain significant to a majority of its citizens. Only 3 percent of Iranians are Ar-abs, compared to 51 percent who are of Persian descent. Al-though Arab Iranians are a minority, the connections Iran has to Arabic nations has prompted a debate among Iranians as to whether they ought to ignore or embrace the Arabic part of their culture.

The nation now known as Iran did not receive that name until 1935, when its ruler at the time, Reza Shah Pahlavi, or-dered the change. Until then it was Persia, a country with a long and illustrious history. The kingdom of Persia was the most powerful in the world for nearly twelve hundred years, beginning with its establishment in 550 B.C. by Cyrus the Great. In his book *The Persian Puzzle*, Kenneth M. Pollack writes, "In 522 B.C., when Cambyses' son Darius ascended the throne as the king of kings of Persia, his empire was the greatest in the world. It stretched from the Aegean to Afghanistan, from the Black Sea to the Blue Nile. It was estimated to have contained 50 million people." The Persian Empire stood until it was conquered by Islamic armies in A.D. 640. Even then, however, the Persian influence remained strong. According to Pollack, the new Muslim rulers retained the Persian monetary system and many of Persia's practices, including the veiling of women. The Persian language, known as Farsi, continued to be spoken alongside Arabic, and it was not until the ninth century that Islam became the predominant religion. Iranians continue to observe the Zoroastrian New Year, even though that once-dominant religion has long been a minority faith.

Despite Islam being the religion of nearly all Iranians, many Iranians disdain being lumped together with their Middle Eastern neighbors. They point out that their heritage is different from others' in the Middle East. S. Rob Sobhani, writing for OpinionJournal.com, asserts, "Iranians are not Arabs and their whole frame of reference, historical and cultural, is Persian." In fact, the very name Iran points to the country's unique background. It means "land of the Aryans." Prior to its co-opting by Nazi Germany, who considered Aryans to be non-Jewish white Europeans, *Aryans* merely meant people who were Indo-Iranian. Some Iranians are so displeased with being associated with Arab culture that they take steps to distance themselves from it. Bahman Aghai Diba, writing for the *Persian Journal*, argues that not only are Iranians not Arabs, but that they should "show that Iran is a country different from [the nations of the] Arabs from all points of view." Diba suggests that Iranians make this clear by taking steps such as removing Arabic words from their speech.

However, many people disagree with Iranians who define themselves solely as Persians and ignore the nation's Islamic and Arabic history. In a column for the Web site Iranian.com, Roozbeh Shirazi writes, "These people exhibit a xenophobic mentality that seems comfortable attributing all of Iran's ills and misfortune to the Arabs and Islam, while forgetting that the hybridization of different cultures created new scientific advances, art, and literature." Other Iranians argue that by showing disdain for Arabs, Iranians are belittling their own culture and hampering relations within the Middle East. According to Shadi Akhavan, also writing for Iranian.com, Iranians who speak ill of Arabs are "contributing to the sense of friction . . . that [has] made it so difficult for the Middle Eastern countries to work together in the first place."

Iran's heritage makes it unique among the Islamic nations of the Middle East, but it faces many of the same concerns, such as conflict with the United States and Europe over the treatment of its citizens. The authors in *Opposing Viewpoints: Iran* consider the issues facing Iran in the following chapters: Is Iran a Threat to Global Security? What Is the State of Human Rights in Iran? How Should the United States Respond to Iran? and What Is the Future of Iran? It remains to be seen whether Iran's Persian past will have any impact on these issues.

OPPOSING
VIEWPOINTS®
SERIES

CHAPTER 1

Is Iran a Threat to Global Security?

Chapter Preface

Iran is one of the world's leaders in oil production, producing 4.1 million barrels of crude oil per day; it is outpaced by only Saudi Arabia, Russia, and the United States. Furthermore, Iran has more than 100 billion barrels in reserve, third only to Iraq and Saudi Arabia. Thus, should Iran choose to do so, it could use its oil as leverage over oil-needy countries with which it has political disagreements. In particular, Iran might choose to pull its oil off the market should the conflict between it and other nations over its plans to develop nuclear power, and possibly nuclear weapons, escalate.

The United States has not purchased oil from Iran since the Islamic Revolution in 1979, so it would not be directly affected by a removal of Iranian oil from the world market. However, Iran's actions could cause a significant increase in the price of oil for all nations. The price of oil was approximately sixty dollars per barrel in March 2006, and commentators suggest that that price could nearly double should Iran pull its oil off the market. The editors of the *Washington Times* write, "A crisis with Iran that removed millions of barrels per day from the world market could send the world oil price well beyond the $100 level, possibly tipping the world into a recession whose depth and duration are unknowable." Because oil is so important to most nations, the lack of it could lead not only to economic troubles but to military conflict as well; the quest for oil has often been blamed for starting wars.

Not everyone believes that Iran will remove its oil from the market as a way of expressing anger toward actions taken by the United States, Europe, and the United Nations over its nuclear plans. However, Iran may make decisions that cause similar consequences. One possibility, suggested by Ian Bremmer, a senior fellow at the World Policy Institute, is that Iran could threaten the movement of oil tankers within the Strait of Hormuz, a body of water controlled by Iran. In a worst-case scenario, that action could shut down the Persian Gulf oil supply.

Iran's oil minister has claimed that Iran will not reduce the amount of oil it exports. However, as its president, Mahmoud Ahmadinejad, has observed, the relationship between Iran and the nations that purchase its oil is not symbiotic. He has been quoted as saying, "Energy is a matter for the West; . . . any decision in this regard will not hurt us. It will hurt the consumers and not the producers." Ahmadinejad's stance points to the ability Iran has to pose a significant threat to global security. The authors in the following chapter consider the potential danger of Iran to the United States and the rest of the world.

| *"When Iran has the bomb, it will not
| have respect for anyone."*

Iran Is a Nuclear Threat

Douglas Davis

*In the following viewpoint Douglas Davis argues that Iran will
soon be capable of producing nuclear weapons. According to
Davis, Iran's ability to develop these weapons has been aided by
Russia, which has given Iran nuclear technologies. He asserts
that Iran may decide to use nuclear arms to attack Israel and establish Islamic dominance throughout the world. Davis is the
London correspondent for the* Jerusalem Post *and a contributor
to the* Spectator, *a British weekly magazine.*

As you read, consider the following questions:

1. According to the author, what slogan was once inscribed
   on Iran's missiles?
2. What "fatal mistake" have European negotiators made,
   in Davis's view?
3. According to the author, what did Iran learn from
   Israel's attack on an Iraqi nuclear reactor?

The Middle East is on the brink of going nuclear, and the
rest of the world is fiddling or looking the other way. The

United States is draining its energies in Iraq, the Europeans are fussing over 'soft power' diplomacy, and the UN [United Nations] monitoring agencies are dithering. 'We are not asking the tough questions,' a senior official in the Vienna-based UN nuclear-monitoring industry told me [in January 2005]. 'We are not being persistent. We are too afraid to offend. We are failing.'

One of the problems is that the Americans have lost credibility over [Iraq's] supposed weapons of mass destruction. But my Vienna source is less concerned that Washington was wrong in Iraq than that the UN monitoring agencies are afflicted by creeping paralysis in Iran. At a moment of global crisis, relations between America and the UN nuclear inspectorate are poisonous, with George W. Bush actively seeking to curtail the tenure of Mohamed El-Baradei, the largely ineffective head of the International Atomic Energy Agency (IAEA).

Israel's Knowledge

All this has complicated the attempt to deal with the clutch of states in the Middle East that are understood to be rushing headlong down the nuclear route. Who, now, would believe fresh alarums from Washington about another rogue state—a member of the Axis of Evil, no less—that is on the brink of going nuclear? Only the Israelis, it seems.

Israel's senior intelligence and military officials have already produced a chilling countdown to Iran's imminent emergence as a nuclear power: by spring 2005 Iran will have acquired a fully independent research and development capability; by 2007 it will have reached the 'point of no return,' and by 2008 it will have produced its first nuclear weapon.

Israeli officials appear particularly well qualified to judge these developments: their secret signal-intelligence Unit 8200 is reported to have cracked the sophisticated Iranian code that enabled Israel to eavesdrop on communications between Iran and its nuclear suppliers over several years.

Israel itself is a veteran of the nuclear club, but its weapons are labelled 'deterrence-only' and would not be rolled out unless Israel faced a doomsday scenario. Some of its neighbours might be less inhibited. Senior Israeli intelligence sources I spoke to [in January 2005] have no doubt that Iran is intent on acquiring nuclear weapons. And while his masters dither, my source in Vienna is equally adamant that the world is facing a real and present danger. 'You only switch off the monitoring systems, as Iran did in 2002, if you have something to hide.' But he, like the Israelis, is also worried about what might be going on in Egypt, Syria and Saudi Arabia, just three of about 18 countries—mostly Muslim and ore-rich African states—where nuclear scientist Dr Abdul Qadeer Khan has left his fingerprints.

Drikhan's Influence

A.Q. Khan, who delivered the 'Islamic bomb' to Pakistan, ran a vast global network of front companies, manufacturers and middlemen to facilitate his entrepreneurial activities, now regarded as the most serious case of proliferation in history. He was eventually rumbled by Western intelligence agencies in October 2003 when a Libya-bound freighter stuffed with Malaysian-made nuclear products was seized.

Confronted with the evidence, [Libyan ruler] Muammar Gaddafi fessed up, and the Americans found themselves with a trove that included tons of nuclear equipment, including 4,000 centrifuges for enriching uranium, the blueprints for a 10-kiloton atomic bomb and enough information about the good doctor to further whet their collective appetite. After a partial admission—that he had also dealt with Iran and North Korea—A.Q. Khan disappeared and [Pakistani] President Pervaiz Musharraf refused all requests, including those from Washington, to question him about his dealings in other states.

The reason he is incommunicado—and that President Musharraf shields him so zealously—is a matter of intense

Walt Handelsman. Reproduced by permission.

speculation, not least because it is unlikely that A.Q. Khan could have ploughed such a sensitive field, on such a scale, so lucratively and for so long without attracting high-level attention at home. But President Musharraf is an American ally in the war on terrorism and the CIA [Central Intelligence Agency] must restrain itself. It is safe to assume, however, that the intelligence agencies' most urgent questions relate to Iran. As with Libya, A.Q. Khan is said to have provided [Iran] not only with equipment for enriching uranium, but also with actual designs for the bomb.

Not a Peaceful Effort

The Russians added the icing. Their contribution has gone far beyond helping to construct Iran's ostensibly peaceful Bushehr reactor. It is clear, said one Israeli intelligence source, that without the transfer of nuclear technologies from Russia, Iran could not have achieved the pace of progress that it has in developing nuclear weapons. Would [Iran] use them? Iran is not the only country in the world that is governed by Islamic law, actively nurtures Islamic terrorists and has a problem relating to the non-Islamic world. Uniquely, though, it has pledged to destroy a fellow UN member: Israel. The rhetoric of the mullahs was encapsulated in a five-word slogan inscribed on Iran's Shihab-3 missiles when they were paraded through Tehran on Revolution Day in 2003—'Israel must be wiped out.'

This is a danger which my Vienna source—neither Jewish nor, indeed, Western—believes is most acute. Israel is facing a very serious threat, he says, and the nuclear-monitoring industry has 'utterly failed to address the profound and legitimate concerns it has about its national security'. A senior Israeli intelligence source echoes the anxiety. With the characteristic caution of his craft, he estimates that 'since the Iranians are so bent on the destruction of Israel, there is a probability that they will use their nuclear weapons aggressively against Israel'.

Like others in the field, he is contemptuous of Iran's claim to be pursuing nuclear energy for strictly peaceful purposes. It simply does not add up. Iran possesses among the largest proven oil and gas reserves in the world, more than enough to fuel its domestic needs. Why would it opt for nuclear energy, which is far more complicated to develop and far more expensive to produce?

Further, the Israeli source links Iran's quest for nuclear weapons to its greater ambitions for leadership, not only in the region, but throughout the wider Islamic world. In other words, while existing nuclear powers acquired their devastating capability for defence and deterrence, Iran might intend using its nuclear weapons to project its power in the cause of its geopolitical objective—Islamic dominance and, ultimately, a global Islamic state.

A Dangerous Situation

The problems with Iran, says my Vienna source, are compounded by an acute inferiority complex. Iran does, indeed, labour under two inherent disabilities: firstly, it is a non-Arab state in a predominantly Arab region; secondly, it is rooted in Islam's minority Shia stream. But these handicaps are unlikely to inhibit its march to power. The combined strength of its other assets—its vast oil and gas reserves, its uncompromising religious zeal, its driving political ambition coupled with a nuclear-capable military machine—would make it an irresistible force. The mullahs would be propelled to centre stage in the Middle East, the wider Muslim world, and also in the international arena. My Vienna source cautions that 'when Iran has the bomb, it will not have respect for anyone'.

Can Iran's race to nuclear weapons be halted? The experts shudder and look with alarm at the dithering IAEA and the naive efforts of a detumescent European Union. So far, the earnest applications of 'soft diplomacy' by Britain, France and Germany have achieved negligible results. As with the weapons inspectors, duplicity is the name of the game for Iran's skillful negotiators, who run rings around the European infidels sent to buy them off. Agreements that are locked up on Monday night somehow escape by Tuesday morning. The German foreign minister, Joschka Fischer, acknowledges that 'the nuclearisation of Iran will have consequences for the whole region—and for European security'. But he concedes that 'up to now, Europe has delivered nothing'.

The grim reality is that Iran provided the test-bed for a European-style solution, complete with high diplomacy, economic incentives and multilateral institutions. Having been handed a mandate by Washington to stop Iran, Europe appears to have comprehensively failed. Iran not only continues to use its hundreds of centrifuges to enrich uranium in breach of 'agreements', but it is also using laser enrichment and it is processing plutonium, an alternative nuclear fuel source. In the language of the trade, it has taken the 'plutogenic' route.

Europe's Mistake

The fatal mistake that the European negotiators appear to have made is to project their own values on to Iran's leaders, assuming that revolutionary mullahs share the aspirations and impulses of rational decision-makers in the West (Would it ever occur to any Western leader to send waves of children running through minefields, as Iranian children did in the Iran-Iraq war, in order to clear the danger?).

Iran's political compass is fixed on a symbiosis of ideology and religion, which imbues its decisions with a mystical, transcendental supernaturalism, beyond the experience and understanding of conventional Western political thought and practice. No surprise, then, that the clutch of economic carrots dangled by secular, democratic, liberal Europe cuts little ice in revolutionary Tehran, which has its sights set on divine destiny.

'We try to engage them as far as we can,' says Joschka Fischer, 'and if the Americans joined us, that would make it much more powerful.' But it is clear that the Americans have their hands full. And in any case, George W. Bush is contemptuous of Europe's enthusiasm for a 'critical dialogue' with a side-serving of containment-lite which, in Mr Fischer's view, should not be supported by military or economic consequences. While the hapless Fischer insists that 'we must do everything to contain the threat', what he really seems to be saying is that we must learn to live with the Iranian bomb.

But is the German foreign minister right to imply nothing can be done? It is true that economic sanctions will have the effect of driving oil prices through the ceiling. It is also true that military action, like Israel's 1981 air strike, which destroyed Iraq's Osirak reactor—and, with it, [Iraqi leader] Saddam Hussein's nuclear weapons programme—will not be easy. The Iranians have learned the lesson of Osirak. Their nuclear facilities are widely dispersed in scores of sites throughout the country—above ground, underground and, most problematically, in civilian population centres. It would be hideously difficult to destroy them all. But nothing less will do.

VIEWPOINT 2

> "While Iran is seriously threatened by
> the U.S. and [Israel], Iran only threat-
> ens the possibilities of self-defense."

Iran Is Not a Nuclear Threat

Edward S. Herman

*In the following viewpoint Edward S. Herman contends that
Iran is not a nuclear threat to the United States and Israel but is
instead threatened by those two nations. Herman maintains that
the American media has helped the U.S. government make Iran
appear a legitimate target of aggression by spreading propaganda
about Iran's nuclear ambitions while ignoring America's and
Israel's nuclear weapons. Herman is a professor emeritus of finance at the Wharton School of Economics at the University of
Pennsylvania and an author whose works include* The Real Terror Network.

As you read, consider the following questions:

1. What comparison does Herman make between Guatemala and Iraq?
2. What is the "first rule in supportive propaganda," according to the author?
3. What is the basic premise of David Sanger's article, in
   Herman's opinion?

Edward S. Herman, "Iran's Dire Threat," *Z Magazine*, October 2004, vol. 17, no. 10.
Reproduced by permission.

Iran is the next U.S. and Israeli target, so the mainstream U.S. media are once again serving the state agenda by focusing on Iran's alleged menace and refusing to provide context that would show the menace to be pure Orwell [dystopian fiction]—that is, while Iran is seriously threatened by the U.S. and its aggressively ethnic-cleansing client [Israel], Iran only threatens the possibilities of self-defense.

Comical Claims

You might have thought that after the retrospectively awkward and embarrassing media service to Bush's lies about [Iraqi leader Saddam Hussein's] weapons of mass destruction and dire threat to U.S. national security, which greased the skids to the invasion/occupation of Iraq, that the media would be less prone to jump uncritically on war propaganda bandwagons. But you would be wrong. It is a pretty reliable law of media performance that whenever the state targets an enemy, the media will get on the bandwagon enthusiastically or, at minimum, allow themselves to be mobilized as agents of propaganda and disinformation. Given the power of the United States and the extreme weakness of its usual targets, the claims of the fearsome threat posed by the targets are always comical. My favorite remains Guatemala in the early 1950s, when the National Security Council [NSC] claimed that this poor, tiny, and effectively disarmed country was "increasingly [an] instrument of Soviet aggression in this hemisphere" and was posing a security threat to the United States as well as its neighbors. As in the case of Iraq in 2002–2003, most of the neighbors failed to recognize the dire threat and had to be bribed and coerced into supporting the U.S. position, and the UN [United Nations] had to be (and was) neutralized.

In fact, the Communists hadn't taken over Guatemala and, with U.S. direct and indirect assistance, it was invaded and occupied by a U.S.-organized band of expatriates and mercenaries a month after the dire claims by the NSC. The *New York*

Times and mass media in general cooperated fully in the propaganda campaign that made this proxy aggression palatable to the public. This early "liberation" transformed a democracy into an authoritarian counterinsurgency and terror state. The *Times* has never apologized for this performance and it has carefully avoided analyzing the results of that earlier intervention and contrasting it with the government's (and its own) pre-invasion propaganda claims.

Manipulation and Propaganda

Several decades later, in the 1980s, Nicaragua provided a partial rerun of the Guatemala experience, with an alleged dire security threat based on a link of the leftist Sandinistas to Moscow, a link mainly forced by an arms boycott and open U.S. campaign of destabilization, subversion, and sponsored terrorism. There was once again an army of expatriates organized and funded by the U.S.—the contras—that engaged in systematic terrorism. Once again the neighbors of Nicaragua couldn't see the dire threat and spent a great deal of effort in trying to fend off the United States by mediation and proposed compromises, which the [Ronald] Reagan administration resented and shunted aside. Once again, an appeal to the UN for protection against intervention by violence was futile and an International Court finding against the United States was ignored. In this case, the United States was able to oust the Sandinistas by the combination of terrorism and boycott, which halved per capita incomes, and by the effective manipulation of an election, in which the United States intervened with advice, money, propaganda, and a blackmail threat—only if the Sandinistas were ousted would the boycott and sponsored terrorism be terminated. The combination worked and the Sandinistas were ousted.

The mainstream media carefully avoided the Guatemala context as they once again served as agents of state propaganda, demonizing the Sandinistas, failing to contest the stream of lies justifying the violent intervention, ignoring its gross illegality, declaring the 1984 Nicaraguan election a "sham" (*New York Times*), whereas the genuine sham elections held in El Salvador in 1982 and 1984 under conditions of severe state terror were declared promising steps toward democracy (see [Edward S.] Herman and [Noam] Chomsky, *Manufacturing Consent*; note also how the U.S. media is now finding the U.S.-appointed puppet government of Iraq a democratic breakthrough: "Early Steps, Maybe, Toward a Democracy in Iraq," *NYT*, July 27, 2004). When the terror war, blackmail, and other forms of electoral intervention successfully removed the Sandinistas, the media were ecstatic, the *New York Times* featuring David Shipler's ode to "Victory Through Fair Play."

Vilifying Iran

So just as Guatemala, Nicaragua, and Iraq were dire threats, so is Iran today because the Bush government says so and is supported here by [Israeli prime minister] Ariel Sharon. The first rule in supportive propaganda is to intensify attention to the villain and the alleged threat that he poses. Thus, the claims that Iran is trying to become a nuclear power have become the continuous basis of news, with all the details and claims of its moves toward nuclear capability newsworthy, emanating as they are from a superpower that is a primary-definer-plus. When it barks, all the smaller doggies in the "international community," including [UN head] Kofi Annan and relevant UN agency officials (in this case, Dr. Mohamed ElBaradei, director general of the International Atomic Energy Agency [IAEA]), join in with their complementary barks. Nevertheless, Dr. ElBaradei has been uncomfortable in his role of UN agency frontperson for the U.S. buildup toward an attack on Iran, his role being similar to that of Hans Blix in the preparation for the Iraq attack. In a recent interview with *Al-Ahram News* (July 27, 2004), he notes how confined he is by his limited powers, so that he cannot visit Israel's Dimon reactor,

No Intention to Attack

Iran continues to sponsor terrorism, although not against the West. It was an Iranian-made arsenal that was found on the *Karine A*, the ship caught by Israel on a smuggling run, allegedly to the Palestinian Authority, possibly to Hezbollah. . . .

Yet should this mean that Iran is just Iraq with one of the letters changed? Absolutely not. Except in the minds of the most hysterical hawks, a capability does not constitute a threat. A threat arises when there is capability plus intention. And there is no evidence that Iran has the intention to attack us. Iran's relative flaunting of its nuclear ambitions may even, in one sense, be reassuring: it suggests that the bomb is regarded as a deterrent, or perhaps even a bargaining chip, rather than as an offensive weapon.

Andrew Gilligan, Spectator, November 27, 2004.

only Iran's facilities, although he believes the only real solution is denuclearization throughout the Middle East (www.iaea.org).

The analogy with the attention to Iraq's alleged possession and threat of weapons of mass destruction in 2001–2003 is close: The United States made those claims, pressed them on the UN and its allies, and in consequence this became first order news. Today, the United States makes charges against Iran, presses its allies and the IAEA, and this makes the issue newsworthy. As a crude index, during the last six months (February 27–August 27, 2004), the *New York Times* had 21 articles whose headlines indicated that their subject matter was Iran's threat to acquire nuclear capability, with dozens more mentioning the Iran-nuclear connection.

The second rule in supportive propaganda is to frame the issues in such a way that the premises of the propaganda source are taken as given, with any inconvenient considerations ignored and any sources that would contest the party line bypassed or marginalized. This technique is well illustrated in David Sanger's "Diplomacy Fails to Slow Advance of Nuclear Arms," the front-page feature article in the *New York Times* of August 8, 2004—a virtually perfect model of propaganda service.

An Example of Propaganda

The frame of Sanger's article is the threat of the nuclear ambitions of Iran and North Korea, the efforts to contain that threat via diplomacy, the difficulties encountered in these efforts, U.S. and Israeli concerns over the matter, and the opinions of Western officials and experts over what should be done. All seven quoted sources in Sanger's piece are present or former U.S. officials, which allows the establishment frame to be presented without challenge.

A basic Sanger premise is that the United States and Israel are good and do not pose threats worthy of mention, so that any "advance" in nuclear arms, or the possession and threat of use of such weapons by these states, is outside the realm of discourse. Thus, the ongoing and well-funded U.S. program of developing "blockbuster" and other tactical nuclear weapons, the Bush plan to make nuclear weapons not merely a deterrent, but usable in normal warfare, and the U.S. intention to exploit space as a platform for nuclear as well as other technologically advanced weapons systems, do not fall under the heading "advance of nuclear arms" and they are not mentioned in the article. These are not the views of the global majority, but they represent the official U.S. view, hence serving as a premise of the *Times* reporter.

A second and related Sanger premise is that the United States has the right to decide who can and cannot have nuclear arms and to compel the disarmament of any country that acquires them. He quotes Bush's statement that he will not "tolerate" North Korea or Iran acquiring such arms, and Sanger treats the U.S. push to keep its targets disarmed as an undebatable position.

A third premise is that while Iran's possible violation of its commitments under the Non-Proliferation Treaty is newsworthy and important, the failure of the United States to follow through on its promise in signing that treaty to work toward the elimination of nuclear weapons through good faith negotiations, a commitment brazenly violated in the open Bush effort to improve and make usable nuclear weapons, is not newsworthy. Again, this is what a press arm of the government would take as a premise, and so does the *New York Times* (and virtually the entire corporate media).

Israel and Iran Are Treated Unequally

A fourth premise of Sanger's piece is that Israel's refusal to have anything to do with the Non-Proliferation Treaty and its possession and threat to use nuclear arms is not relevant as context in discussing the threat of Iran's nuclear capability. Israel is referred to by Sanger only as fearing the Iran threat and possibly planning on preemptive action to eliminate that threat. The Arab states and most of the world cannot see the justice of Israel being allowed to acquire nuclear arms, even with superior conventional forces and a U.S. protective umbrella, while Arab states cannot do so. Again, as Israel is a U.S. client state whose acquisition of nuclear arms was facilitated and is protected by the United States, this matter is outside the orbit of discourse for U.S. officials and hence of the *New York Times* (etc.).

A fifth premise, implicit in the foregoing, is that Iran does not have a right to self-defense. Israel claims that its nuclear weapons are for self-defense in a hostile environment, but Iran, threatened by both Israel and its superpower ally, does not have that right, although its self-defense needs are far more serious than either Israel's or the U.S.'s. This was a premise of officials, and hence of the *New York Times*, in dealing with Guatemala's attempt to buy arms back in 1953, Nicaragua's similar efforts in the 1980s, and Saddam's mythical threatening WMD [weapons of mass destruction] in 2002–3.

Sanger's article is clean in the sense that there is no deviation from the party line on the source of any nuclear threat and the "advances" that are worrisome. The *Times'* subservience to the state in the propaganda buildup to the invasion-occupation of Iraq was not new and was not terminated by that sad experience. On the contrary, it proceeds apace, with any lessons or qualms overpowered by institutional forces that press it to support state crimes now just as it did in the case of the overthrow of democracy in Guatemala in 1954 and other alleged "liberations."

> "Iran's efforts to develop nuclear weapons and its long-standing animosity toward Israel pose a serious danger to that nation."

Iran Is a Threat to Israel

Martin Indyk

The declaration by Iranian president Mahmoud Ahmadinejad that Israel must be destroyed should not be ignored, Martin Indyk contends in the following viewpoint. According to Indyk, although Iran's military is not as powerful as the Israeli army, Iran's efforts to develop nuclear weapons and its long-standing animosity toward Israel pose a serious danger to that nation. In addition, he argues that Iran has already proven to be a threat to Israel through its support of the terrorist organizations Hezbollah and Palestine Islamic Jihad, both of which have orchestrated numerous attacks against Israeli civilians. Indyk is a former U.S. ambassador to Israel and the director of the Saban Center for Middle East Policy at the Brookings Institution in Washington, D.C.

As you read, consider the following questions:

1. What is the major difference between the views expressed by Gamal Abdel Nasser and Mahmoud Ahmadinejad, according to Indyk?

Martin Indyk, "Iran's Bluster Isn't a Bluff," *Los Angeles Times*, November 1, 2005. Reproduced by permission.

2. According to the author, how did Iran utilize Hezbollah and Palestine Islamic Jihad during the 1990s?

3. What did the Ayatollah Khamenei and Ramadan Shallah proclaim, as quoted by Indyk?

Mahmoud Ahmadinejad, the new president of Iran, declared [in October 2005] that "Israel must be wiped off the map."

It was a truly "retro" moment, conjuring up images of Egypt's Gamal Abdel Nasser, who, almost four decades earlier, called on the Arab people to "throw Israel into the sea."

Now, as then, the international community gasped at the lack of civility but could not imagine that the leader who uttered these words was serious. Iran's diplomats were quick to explain it away, and even Ahmadinejad ultimately sought to tone down his words with less inflammatory rhetoric.

But the fact remains, as Ahmadinejad himself pointed out, that his comments were hardly new. In threatening the destruction of Israel, he noted he was only repeating the 27-year-long stance of the Iranian revolution.

There is one important difference between Nasser and Ahmadinejad: Nasser's Egypt was right next door to Israel. In fact, he issued his threat as he sent his army into the Sinai Peninsula and precipitated the 1967 Six-Day War. Ahmadinejad, by contrast, would have to send the Iranian army 1,000 miles across the Persian Gulf and the Arabian desert before he could hope to fulfill his threat.

Iran's Nuclear Goals

It's true that Iran put a huge effort into developing long-range missiles with the ability to strike Israel. But so far, Iran can only load them with chemical warheads. To launch them against the powerful Israeli military would bring disproportionate death and destruction down on Ahmadinejad's own people.

So, does Israel really need to fear the populist ranting of an Iranian hothead president, who seems only to be using Israel as a whipping boy to stir up support for his already faltering government? Shouldn't Israel be satisfied that he scored an own-goal, further isolating Iran and placing its actions under greater international scrutiny?

The answer to my mind is clearly no. There is plenty of International Atomic Energy Agency evidence to indicate that Iran is bent on acquiring a nuclear weapons capability and that this goal is broadly supported by all of Iran's political factions. [In 2001], another Iranian leader, the supposedly moderate Hashemi Rafsanjani, provided the strategic rationale for using nuclear weapons. He explained that in a nuclear exchange, Iran could withstand a second strike, whereas "the use of a nuclear bomb against Israel will leave nothing on the ground."

Now Ahmadinejad has explained Iran's ideological rationale, justifying his threat to Israel in the context of Islam's centuries-long struggle against the infidel. He also threatened Arab leaders who might think of signing treaties that recognized Israel, just as during the Oslo [peace] process, Ayatollah Ali Khamenei, Iran's supreme religious leader, issued a fatwa to assassinate [Palestinian leader] Yasser Arafat.

Some will point out that Iran appears to be at least five years from acquiring nuclear weapons and that the international community has already mobilized to prevent that from happening.

Iran Supports Terrorism Against Israel

But that argument overlooks Iran's other weapon against Israel: Its ongoing war by proxy, which it has been waging for more than a decade. Iran's primary proxies are two terrorist organizations: Hezbollah, which operates out of southern Lebanon, and Palestine Islamic Jihad, which carries out terrorist operations against Israeli civilians. The Iranian intelligence service trains, funds, arms and directs both.

Gary Brookins. Reproduced by permission.

In the 1990s, Iran was able to use these proxies in its attempt to thwart the Clinton administration's peacemaking efforts. Their attacks did much to defeat Shimon Peres in the 1996 Israeli elections, which led to the stalling of the peace process. Subsequently, Hezbollah's success in forcing Israel's unilateral withdrawal from southern Lebanon in May 2000 helped provide the rationale for the Palestinian intifada, which then destroyed the peace process.

After Israel withdrew from southern Lebanon, Hezbollah immediately turned its attention to supporting Palestinian terror attacks in Israel (giving the lie to the idea that it was just a Lebanese resistance movement). Iran's backing for this effort was starkly revealed in January 2002 with the interception of the *Karine A*, a ship smuggling a huge cache of Iranian arms from the Persian Gulf to Gaza.

Once Iran's proxy war shifted from Lebanon to the West Bank and Gaza, however, Islamic Jihad moved into the vanguard position. Its activities were barely distinguishable from the suicide bombings undertaken by [Palestinian terrorist organization] Hamas. Nevertheless, during the intifada, Hamas was on several occasions willing to pause for tactical reasons. On each occasion, the fragile calm would be punctured by an Islamic Jihad attack that provoked Israeli retaliation, which would then bring Hamas back into the fray. In this way, Iran was able to keep the intifada boiling until Palestinians could take it no longer.

Interfering with the Cease-Fire

Even now, when more than 80% of Palestinians want the current calm to continue, Iran is pushing Islamic Jihad to provoke violence. In the nine months since an informal cease-fire took hold, Islamic Jihad has been responsible for all four of the major suicide bombings that have punctured the relative quiet, including the one in Hadera [in October 2005.]

Lest anyone doubt the Iranian hand in guiding this effort, in September 2005, Khamenei made a public display of meeting with Ramadan Abdullah Shallah, the head of Islamic Jihad, to claim credit for Israel's disengagement from Gaza. Khamenei and Shallah proclaimed that "jihad is the only way to confront the Zionist enemy."

Ahmadinejad's declaration, therefore, is certainly no aberration. It was just one of those moments when the world could no longer avoid noticing Iran's decades-long aggression toward the Jewish State. Were Israel not to take these threats seriously, it would be as foolish as Ahmadinejad.

| "A nuclearized Iran is extremely unlikely to pose an existential threat to Israel."

Iran Is Not a Threat to Israel

Ehsaneh I. Sadr

In the following viewpoint Ehsaneh I. Sadr argues that Iran is unlikely to launch a nuclear attack against Israel. According to Sadr, Iran's leaders understand that launching nuclear weapons at Israel could lead to that nation responding with a similar attack. Sadr further argues that Iran has little reason to give nuclear arms to terrorist organizations that target Israel. At the time this viewpoint was written, Sadr was a graduate student in the Department of Government and Politics at the University of Maryland in College Park.

As you read, consider the following questions:

1. According to Sadr, what is the first reason given for why Iran's leaders may not understand the doctrine of mutually assured destruction?

2. Why does the author believe it is unlikely that Iran would transfer nuclear weapons to terrorist organizations?

Ehsaneh I. Sadr, "The Impact of Iran's Nuclearization on Israel," *Middle East Policy*, vol. 12, no. 2, Summer 2005. Copyright © 2005 Basil Blackwell Ltd. Reproduced by permission of Blackwell Publishers.

3. In Sadr's view, why is an Iran that possesses nuclear weapons less likely to support anti-Israel terrorist groups?

Iran's attainment of nuclear weapons might threaten the very existence of Israel as a Jewish state in at least three conceivable ways. First, Iran might launch a nuclear weapon directly at Israel. Second, Iran might transfer nuclear weapons to a terrorist organization such as Hezbollah that would launch them toward Israel. Third, Iran might be emboldened to attack Israel by conventional means or through terrorist proxies without fear of retaliation.

There are at least three ways in which one might conceive of Iran launching a nuclear warhead directly at Israel: (1) if the Cold War–proven doctrine of MAD [mutually assured destruction] failed to work in the context of the Middle East, and the Iranian government purposefully and consciously chose to bomb Israel; (2) if a fanatical "rogue" element within the current regime gained control over and launched nuclear weapons; or (3) if the regime fell apart entirely and Iran's new and fanatical rulers decided to bomb Israel.

The Principles of MAD

In a [summer] 1979 [*International Security*] article critical of the lack of strategic thinking in U.S. nuclear policy, Colin Gray laid out the central and paradoxical principles of MAD:

> Strategic nuclear war, presumably, is deterred by the prospect of the employment of [nuclear] forces; while, should a war actually occur, again presumably, each side executes its largely preplanned sequence of more and more punishing strike options . . . and then dies with the best grace it can muster.

It seems counterintuitive that war could be deterred by the presence of weapons which can never be used out of fear of the destructive power they would surely unleash on one's own society. Yet, the MAD doctrine has served the world quite well, not only during the Cold War but also in the Sino-Soviet and India-Pakistan cases. Given MAD's spotless track record, one might reasonably expect it to apply in the Middle East as well. At least three reasons have been given, however, for why MAD logic might escape the Iranian government.

The first reason is that Iran's leaders are unlikely to understand the subtle theoretical arguments and paradoxical principles of the MAD doctrine. Richard Russell argues, [in an article in the August 2004 *Parameters*,] for example, that "[t]he Iranian clerics are not well schooled in the ins and outs of the elaborate Western strategic literature formulated during the Cold War." Similarly, George Perkovich has said [in an April 2003 Carnegie Endowment paper] that "[p]olitical leaders like Khamenei and Rafsanjani see nuclear weapons as an almost magical source of national power and autonomy. These men are political clerics, not international strategists or technologists." The implication is that Iran's leaders have an undeveloped appreciation for nuclear strategies and doctrines and that this deficit leaves them dangerously incapable of rationally calculating the risks of actually using nuclear weapons.

Problematic Analyses

Such an argument is problematic for at least two reasons. First of all, whether Rafsanjani and Khamenei currently understand the details of various nuclear doctrines is less important than whether they can grasp them fairly quickly after joining the nuclear club. Unless we are to succumb to suspiciously ethnocentric—even racist—assumptions regarding the ability of Iranians to learn, there is relief to be found in the example of all the other nuclear states, in which the development of doctrine followed the development of weapons. Second, it is far from clear that a thorough grasp of "the elaborate Western strategic literature" is necessary. Indeed, the most important principle of deterrence requires only a very basic, even primitive, understanding that the launching of nuclear weapons against a nuclearized enemy is sure to be followed by the destruction of one's own cities. The belief that only complicated strategic doctrines can deter the initiation of nuclear warfare may stem more from the scholar's vanity than the policy maker's need.

A second reason given for MAD's irrelevance in the Iranian context is that Iran, as an ideologically driven state, might be willing to tolerate enormous costs, including its own annihilation, for the pleasure of destroying the Jewish state. Indeed, the most pessimistic analyses suggest that the primary driver of Iran's nuclear quest is its plan to actually use the weapons it acquires against "infidels" such as Israel and the United States. A recent report by a group of Israeli defense experts, for example, describes Iran as a "suicide nation" willing to risk its own survival so long as Israel is eliminated in the process.

These pessimistic analyses are generally supported by reference to incendiary statements made by Iranian leaders that indicate a blind hatred for and desire to inflict pain upon and possibly use nuclear weapons against the state of Israel. However, while "Death to Israel" continues to be a popular refrain (especially on Jerusalem Day, the official anti-Israel holiday), threats to actually use nuclear weapons against the Jewish state are extremely difficult to find. . . .

A third reason given for the failure of the MAD doctrine to deter an Iranian nuclear attack against Israel is that the initially small number of weapons in Iran's arsenal would be vulnerable to a preventive Israeli attack. As such, a situation of crisis instability would result in which Iran might rationally choose to attack Israel first. This argument is weakened by two considerations. The first is that (as the geographic dispersal of its nuclear program shows) Iran is likely to minimize its vulnerability by hiding and frequently moving its weapons

Not a Central Objective

The likelihood that Iran will initiate an attack on Israel with nonconventional weapons—once it obtains such a capability—is not high. It is true that of all countries in the region, the Iranian regime has taken the most extreme stand against Israel, and sees its destruction as a solution to the Palestinian problem. Elimination of Israel, however, is not among its central objectives. Any attempt on Iran's part to materialize this goal by using nonconventional weapons is apt to come at a heavy price in economic, military and political terms, primarily via a severe U.S. reaction. Thus, it is more likely that Iran will prefer to reserve its nonconventional warfare capability as an option of last resort against a critical threat.

Ephraim Kam, Strategic Assessment, *October 1998.*

to different locations. The second is that an Israeli neutralization of Iran's nuclear weapons is still less destructive, more easily recovered from, and therefore preferable to Israeli nuclear retaliation to an Iranian first strike. . . .

Rogues and Terrorists

It is also important to consider the possibility that rogue actors within the current government or a revolutionary movement might gain access to and launch nuclear weapons against Israel. The problem of safeguarding nuclear stockpiles against rogue actors is one that all members of the nuclear club have had to deal with. There is no reason to believe that Iranian leaders would be any less apt to guard against such an eventuality than their Chinese, Indian, Russian or even American counterparts. Concern that the Iranians lack the technical skills to do so may be remedied by transfer of the necessary technologies and know-how.

There is reason to believe, however, that the probability of rogue elements attempting to gain access to and launch nuclear weapons may, in fact, be lower in the Islamic Republic than it is in some of the other nuclear countries. . . .

Iran's support for terrorist groups targeting Israel is often cited as evidence of the further dangers its nuclearization would pose. In a Senate hearing on Iran, for example, Senator Russell Feingold stated, "Given the close relationship between powerful elements of the Iranian government and several terrorist organizations, . . . Iran is among the most likely states, if not the most likely state, that could transfer weapons of mass destruction to terrorist organizations." A [November 2003] article by the Arms Control Association also argues that "the presence of fissile materials [in Iran] . . . would pose . . . a danger in terms of proliferation and world terror." The concern is, of course, that Iran might pass nuclear weapons on to the terrorist organizations with which it maintains close ties. Such an event would be particularly worrying for Israel, the primary target of Iranian-backed terrorist groups like Lebanon's Hezbollah.

The likelihood of Iran actually transferring nuclear weapons to a terrorist organization is, however, extremely small for several reasons. Even Hezbollah, the group most closely linked with the Iranian regime, cannot be counted on for 100 percent loyalty. Hezbollah's growing autonomy from the Iranian government can be noted in the 2000 statement by its deputy secretary general that "Iran is different from Lebanon" and in the dwindling presence of the Iranian Republican Guard Corps at one time numbering nearly 1,000. It would be irrational as well as uncharacteristic of the Iranian regime to entrust the most sophisticated and deadly weapon in its arsenal to an independent organization whose allegiance is not guaranteed. . . .

Less Likely to Support Terrorism

A third conceivable danger of Iran's entrance into the nuclear club is that it might be emboldened to attack Israel through conventional means or terrorist proxies with little fear of retaliation. Trusting that the Israelis would not wish to escalate a conflict to the point of nuclear exchange, Iran might perceive itself as having a freer hand to harass Israel by increasing funding for groups like Hezbollah and Islamic Jihad and encouraging additional suicide attacks.

Such an argument hinges on the assumption that the only thing keeping Iran from providing more support to these groups is its current fear of Israeli retaliation. It is far from clear, however, that this is the case. Indeed, Iran's relative transparency regarding its support for Hezbollah over the past 25 years suggests that the government is not at all cowed by possible Israeli retaliation. There are numerous instances of Iranian presidents and supreme leaders issuing public words of support and praise for Hezbollah's actions against Israel. It is more likely that resource constraints and strategic evaluations of spending priorities, rather than fear of Israeli reprisals, dictated the extent of Iranian support for groups advocating the violent overthrow of the Israeli state.

There may, in fact, be reason to believe that a nuclearized Iran would be less likely to continue current levels of support for anti-Israeli terrorist organizations. The most obvious concern is that of nuclear escalation. As proliferation optimists have noted, "The presence of nuclear weapons makes states exceedingly cautious." A frequently cited example is that of India and Pakistan, which some experts believe would have come to more serious blows if not for the introduction of nuclear weapons into their relationship. There is no reason to think that the "nuclear magic" might not be as potent in the context of the Middle East. . . .

A Nuclear Attack Is Unlikely

The above analysis indicates that a nuclearized Iran is extremely unlikely to pose an existential threat to Israel. The doctrine of Mutually Assured Destruction holds in the Iranian context: Iran's clerical rulers, anxious to protect their own power, citizens and civilization, will not launch a war that will lead to their own destruction. Iran's rulers are extremely unlikely to pass nuclear material on to terrorist actors whose loyalty they cannot ensure. They are also unlikely to step up conventional or terrorist harassment of Israel for fear of the escalation of hostilities to nuclear warfare.

> *"Tehran is pursuing a systematic effort to arouse the region against the United States."*

Iranian Anti-Americanism Threatens the United States

A. William Samii

Iranian radio spreads anti-American propaganda both within Iran and throughout the Middle East, A. William Samii asserts in the following viewpoint. According to Samii, Iranian broadcasts make false claims about U.S. foreign policy goals in order to spur Arab resentment toward the United States and undermine peace efforts in the region. Samii is a regional analysis coordinator with Radio Free Europe/Radio Liberty.

As you read, consider the following questions:

1. What did the Voice of the Mujahedin claim about Paul Wolfowitz, according to the author?
2. According to Samii, how did Tehran respond to the presence of American soldiers in Afghanistan?
3. According to the author, what event led to disinformation from Iranian state radio?

In light of Iran's growing political role in Iraq (to say nothing of reports of unofficial activity by Iranian agents), there is cause for concern in the steady stream of anti-American and anti-Coalition[1] propaganda, including inflammatory lies, that continues to flow from Iran to audiences in Iraq and other countries in the region.

Even as a delegation from the Iranian foreign ministry arrived in [Iraq's capital] Baghdad on April 14 [2004] in response to a British request for [Iranian capital] Tehran's help defusing the current unrest, radio and television stations in Iran were sending out messages tailored for Iraq and the rest of the Arabic-speaking world. Thus, on April 13, the Arabic-language Voice of the Mujahedin—which is run by the Iraqi Shiite group the Supreme Council for the Islamic Revolution in Iraq (SCIRI) and transmits from Iran—claimed that the unrest in Iraq is part of a "scenario" launched by "the Zionist lobby that controls the White House." It explained that the closure of Moktada al-Sadr's *Al Hawzah* newspaper and the arrest of al-Sadr's aide are part of a plan to cancel the transfer of power to Iraqis so the United States can stay in the country indefinitely, plunder its oil wealth, and eliminate a culture that does not conform with Israeli interests.

Fanning Hostility

A few days before, on April 8, SCIRI's radio station encouraged violence by speaking of resistance and saying, "The coming days may give many Iraqis a chance to emerge as national heroes." It went on to say that Iraq's foremost Shia religious authority, Ayatollah Ali Sistani, might be forced to issue a decree calling on all Iraqis and Shia to launch a holy war against the Americans.

From the beginning, Tehran has reacted to the American presence in Iraq by fanning hostility to the United States, on state broadcasts as well as those of SCIRI, which until [2003]

1. The coalition government ruling Iraq until a permanent government can be installed.

Spreading Propaganda in Iraq

Even before the [2003] U.S.-led war on Iraq, Iran had begun beaming in Arabic-language television programming in an effort to gain a strategic propaganda foothold in the country—and it has not stopped. Indeed, American labors to win hearts and minds through the television station, al-Iraqiyya, and Radio Sawa have been steadily undermined by these efforts. In April 2003, an Iranian journalist reported that Iranian Revolutionary Guards brought into Iraq radio-transmission equipment, posters, and printed matter for the militia known as the Badr Corps.

Jonathan Schanzer, National Review Online,
May 10, 2004. www.nationalreview.com.

was based in Iran. Virulent commentary is hardly something special in response to the current crisis. On March 31, for example, the Voice of the Mujahedin claimed that if U.S. Deputy Defense Secretary Paul Wolfowitz is appointed ambassador to Iraq he will turn the country "into a base for the Zionist entity." The Zionists, explained the broadcast, want to control all the country's resources and eliminate all national and Islamic symbols. The occupation of Iraq has brought "the Zionist entity" millions of dollars through its participation in Iraq's reconstruction. And a February 10 Voice of the Mujahedin broadcast accused the United States of involvement in a "holocaust" and "genocide" against Iraqis.

This kind of thing is typical of Tehran's broadcasts, heard throughout the Middle East. Like Voice of the Mujahedin, the Arabic service of the official Islamic Republic of Iran Broadcasting can be heard in Baghdad on four AM and FM frequencies. Iran also transmits in Arabic on the 24-hour Al Alam satellite television and on the Sahar television station. Sahar TV carried an interview on March 17 in which there was a discussion of alleged U.S. attempts to settle Jews in Iraq. A series about the destruction of Iraqi cities on Al Alam in March was entitled "The Harvest of One Year of American Occupation."

Iran's Other Targets

Nor are Arabic-speakers the only audience Tehran targets. It has responded to the replacement of the Taliban [regime in Afghanistan] by a pro-American government and the presence of U.S. troops in Afghanistan with a relatively sophisticated multilingual broadcast operation designed to exploit ethnic differences in Afghanistan. This began in December 2001 and continues to this day. Afghanistan's largest minority, the Pashtuns, were the main backers of the Taliban, and Iran's Pashtu-language broadcasts have kept up a constant stream of anti-U.S. insinuation and outright lies that play on ethnic sensitivities and nationalism.

Referring to the late-March unrest in the western Afghan city of Herat, Iranian state radio said in Pashtu on March 30 that locals there were protesting the foreign presence. Another Pashtu-language broadcast that day accused U.S. troops of attacking local Afghan forces in the city of Jalalabad.

A February 2003 Pashtu-language commentary claimed "the majority of experts" believe that the United States is pursuing colonial goals in Afghanistan and Central Asia, and the United States wants to use Afghanistan as a base. Reports of Taliban and al Qaeda [terrorist group] remnants are only a pretext for a long-term U.S. presence, according to the commentary, which concluded by stating, "The lasting presence of American forces in Afghanistan will not only lead to failure to ensure security in this country but also will add to the lack of security and give rise to more confrontations."

One recent event that provoked a rash of disinformation from Iranian state radio was the spate of bombings and attacks in late March in Uzbekistan, just north of Afghanistan.

Commentaries in English and Persian broadcast from north-eastern Iran on March 30 asked who stood to gain from the bombings, and accused the United States of using the violence as a pretext for its military presence in Central Asia. In an added flourish for the Persian-speaking audience, mostly in Afghanistan, the broadcast said that the United States would use the incidents as a pretext for a U.S. presence in southern Asia, adding that the U.S. military presence in Uzbekistan already contributes to insecurity there.

Aiming to Undermine Peace

Finally, the broadcasts accused the United States of opposing Islam. "It can also be predicted at the international level that the U.S.A. may blame the recent terrorist acts in Uzbekistan on Muslims in order to stress that there is a connection between terrorism and Islam and to implement its anti-Islamic plans," Iranian radio claimed in Persian. The broadcast in English accused the United States of having "anti-Islamic policies."

Iranian hostility to the United States is not new, but it has a new twist since the ousters of the Taliban and [Iraq's] Saddam Hussein: Perceiving itself as surrounded by an enemy, Tehran is pursuing a systematic effort to arouse the region against the United States and undermine peace in Iraq and stability elsewhere.

Periodical Bibliography

The following articles have been selected to supplement the diverse views presented in this chapter.

Ali M. Ansari	"A Reality Check on the 'Persian Menace,'" *New Statesman*, February 14, 2005.
Pat Buchanan	"Iran Doesn't Want War with the U.S.," *Conservative Chronicle*, December 8, 2004.
Georgie Anne Geyer	"Bush's Iran Blind Spot," *American Conservative*, September 12, 2005.
Eric S. Margolis	"Iran Builds a Bomb," *American Conservative*, June 21, 2004.
Afshin Molavi	"A New Day in Iran?" *Smithsonian*, March 2005.
William Rusher	"What Shall We Do About Iran?" *Conservative Chronicle*, October 6, 2004.
Chemi Shalev	"Iranian Threat Looms Large in War's 'Day After' Scenario," *Forward*, March 14, 2003.
Stephen Shalom, interviewed by Jason Schulman	"Nukes, the U.S., and Iran," *Democratic Left*, Spring 2005.
Robert Spencer	"Ahmadinejad's Holocaust," *Human Events*, November 7, 2005.
Amir Taheri	"A Clash of Civilizations," *Newsweek International*, September 5, 2005.
Ray Takeyh	"Iran's Nuclear Calculations," *World Policy Journal*, Summer 2003.

OPPOSING
VIEWPOINTS®
SERIES

CHAPTER 2

What Is the State of Human Rights in Iran?

Chapter Preface

Iran is an overwhelmingly Muslim nation. Ninety-seven percent of its inhabitants practice Islam; 89 percent are Shiite Muslims, while the rest are Sunni Muslims. This Islamic majority controls Iran's government, which many observers claim persecutes non-Muslims living within its borders. While all religious minorities in Iran experience some level of religious discrimination, according to the U.S. State Department, adherents of the Baha'i faith are the most persecuted. Baha'is, of which there are between 300,000 and 350,000, are the largest non-Muslim minority in Iran.

The Baha'i faith was founded as an offshoot of Islam in the middle of the nineteenth century. It is a monotheistic religion whose goals include the establishment of a global commonwealth of nations and the elimination of extreme poverty and wealth. Approximately 5 million people worldwide practice Baha'ism. Ironically, it is the faith's connection to Islam that makes it a target of Iran's government, U.S. State Department spokesman Adam Ereli asserts. According to Ereli, "The Government considers Baha'is to be apostates because of their claim to a valid religious revelation subsequent to that of Muhammed [Islam's prophet], despite the fact that Baha'is do not consider themselves to be Muslim."

Iran's antipathy toward Baha'is manifests itself in numerous ways. Unlike other minorities, such as Christians and Jews, Baha'is cannot establish religious schools. They are denied the right to assemble and worship freely and also are barred from government employment. More seriously, hundreds of Baha'is have been killed or imprisoned since the 1979 Iranian revolution; more than two hundred were executed between 1978 and 1998, according to the Baha'i International Community. One death that garnered attention outside Iran, and was condemned by the United States, was that of Zabihullah Mahrami, who died of unknown causes in an Iranian jail. While in prison for ten years because of his faith, he had received numerous death threats.

Religious persecution of Baha'is is one example of the human rights violations many commentators argue are all too common in Iran. The state of human rights in that nation is a serious concern for both its citizens and international observers. In the following chapter the authors debate what freedoms, if any, exist in Iran.

> "The [European Union has] reiterated long-standing human rights concerns [in Iran], including the use of torture ... [and] the use of the death penalty."

Iran Violates Human Rights

Amnesty International

Human rights are largely ignored in Iran, Amnesty International contends in the following viewpoint taken from its 2005 annual report on human rights. The organization asserts that Iranians are subject to torture, religious discrimination, and executions. Amnesty International further details other attacks on human rights, including the imprisonment of journalists who criticize the government and legal discrimination against women. Amnesty International is one of the world's leading human rights watchdog organizations.

As you read, consider the following questions:

1. According to the author, how many candidates were barred from participating in the February 2004 elections in Iran?

2. What was the fate of Hashem Aghajari, as explained by Amnesty International?

Amnesty International, "Amnesty International Annual Report 2005," AMR 51/061/202, www.amnesty.org. © Amnesty International Publications, 1 Easton Street, London WX1X 0DW. Reproduced by permission.

3. According to Amnesty International, how many Iranians were sentenced to flogging in 2004?

A new parliamentary session [in Iran] started in May [2004], following controversial and flawed parliamentary elections in February which were marked by mass disqualification of sitting deputies. The elections resulted in a comprehensive victory for groups opposed to social and political reform. Some of the statements from the new parliamentarians included attacks on women said to be "improperly attired". Incoming women parliamentarians rejected previous policies aimed at gender equality.

The emerging political trend in parliament gave impetus to members of the semi-official Hezbollah, which occasionally attacked gatherings of people they believed supported opposition political movements. It also encouraged the judiciary and its security force to limit public dissent, resulting in arbitrary arrests and the detention of prisoners in secret centres. In the latter half of the year in particular, practices employed by the judiciary—including arbitrary arrest, denial of legal representation and detention in solitary confinement—were responsible for most of the human rights violations reported in the country.

An Ongoing Dialogue

International concern over Iran's obligations to the International Atomic Energy Agency (IAEA) dominated the year [2004]. IAEA reports throughout the year suggested that Iranian officials were not always presenting the entire scope of the country's nuclear programmes. In November, following an agreement with the European Union (EU), Iran committed itself to suspending uranium enrichment.

The ongoing Human Rights Dialogue process between the EU and Iran led to few lasting benefits. In March, the EU stated that it had seen little improvement in human rights and that violations remained widespread. Several Iranian human rights defenders criticized the process for its lack of transparency and effectiveness. In a concluding statement, the EU reiterated long-standing human rights concerns, including the use of torture, unequal rights for women, the use of the death penalty, religious discrimination and the lack of an independent judiciary. Iran's judiciary rejected these comments, while newspaper interviews given by the deputy head of the judiciary, Mohammad Javad Larijani, expressed contempt for the process and [for] human rights.

In November, the UN [United Nations] General Assembly passed a resolution condemning the human rights situation in Iran. It drew attention to Iran's "failure to comply with international standards in the administration of justice, the absence of due process of law, the refusal to provide fair and public hearings and right to counsel . . ." and forms of systematic discrimination. It urged the authorities to appoint an independent and impartial prosecutor in Tehran and to fulfil Iran's international commitments. A proposed visit by the UN Working Group on Enforced or Involuntary Disappearances was postponed at the government's request.

Religions and Political Discrimination

Discriminatory laws and practices continued to be the source of social and political unrest and of human rights violations. People continued to be denied state employment because of their religious affiliation and political opinions under *gozinesh*, or "selection" provisions which serve to prohibit individuals from working for state bodies. Analogous laws applied to professional bodies such as the Bar Association or trade unions.

In January, *gozinesh* criteria were deployed by the Guardians' Council, which reviews laws and policies to ensure that they uphold Islamic tenets and the Constitution, in order to disqualify around 3,500 prospective candidates from standing in the February parliamentary elections. The exclusion of

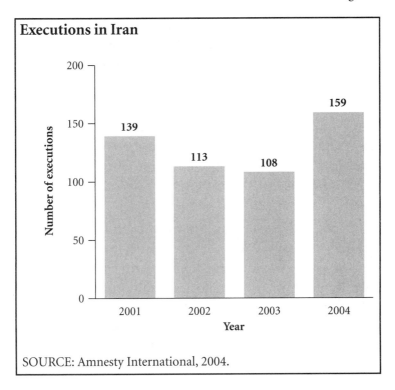

Executions in Iran

SOURCE: Amnesty International, 2004.

around 80 incumbent parliamentarians attracted domestic and international condemnation.

The *gozinesh* provided the legal basis for discriminatory laws and practice. Religious and ethnic groups which were not officially recognized—such as the Bahai's, Ahl-e Haq, Mandaeans (Sabaeans) and Evangelical Christians—were automatically subject to *gozinesh* provisions and faced discrimination in a range of areas, including access to education.

Attacks on Free Speech

Freedoms of expression and association came under attack throughout the year as a result of flagrant flaws in the administration of justice, coupled with a deeply politicized judiciary. Journalists faced politically motivated and arbitrary arrest, prolonged detention, unfair trials and imprisonment. The laws used to arrest and imprison journalists, relating to defamation, national security and disturbing public opinion, were vaguely worded and at variance with international standards. 2004 saw an increase in the harassment or intimidation of the relatives of detainees or people under investigation.

A report published in January by the UN Special Rapporteur on the promotion and protection of the right to freedom of opinion and expression concluded that there was a "climate of fear induced by the systematic repression of people expressing critical views against the authorized political and religious doctrine . . ."

In October and November, scores of journalists, particularly Internet journalists, were arbitrarily detained in connection with their work and especially following publication of an appeal by around 350 signatories, calling for political reform. Those detained were expected to face trial in the following months. They included Javad Gholam Tamayomi, Shahram Rafihzadeh Rouzbeh and Mir Ebrahimi. In December many of those arrested reportedly confessed while in detention, but later told a government body that these confessions were extracted under duress.

Taqi Rahmani, Alireza Alijani and Hoda Saber, intellectuals and writers associated with the National Religious Alliance (Melli Mazhabi), remained arbitrarily detained without any prospect of release. For over a year, the court where they had lodged their appeal had refused to issue a verdict. This effectively prevented the families from taking any form of follow-up action. Despite an announcement in November that they would be released and the payment of substantial bail, the prison authorities prevented them from being released and they remained in detention at the end of the year.

The death sentence passed in 2002 on Professor Hashem Aghajari for statements he made that were construed to be blasphemous was overturned by the Supreme Court in June. However, new charges were brought against him of insulting religious precepts, and "spreading false information". In July,

Professor Hashem Aghajari was sentenced to five years' imprisonment, with two years suspended, and barred from practising his profession for five years. His appeal was still pending before a Tehran court at the end of the year.

Judges Are Not Trusted

Impunity for human rights violations resulted in political instability and mistrust of the judiciary, which was perceived by many human rights activists as unwilling to uphold the law in an impartial manner.

In July, Mohammad Reza Aqdam Ahmadi, a Ministry of Intelligence official, went on trial for participating in the "quasi-intentional murder" of Zahra Kazemi, a photojournalist who died in custody in 2003. He was acquitted following a two-day trial. Following his acquittal, a spokesperson for the judiciary stated that Zahra Kazemi's death must have been an accident, despite forensic reports prepared following her death which indicated that she was murdered. International observers—including UN Special Rapporteurs on freedom of opinion and expression; on the independence of judges and lawyers; and on torture—condemned the flagrantly flawed proceedings. The court ordered the state to pay the family of the deceased the legally required monetary compensation as no culprit had been found. The family lodged an appeal which was pending at the end of the year.

Brothers Manuchehr and Akbar Mohammadi, and Ahmadi Batebi, who were among the students detained, tortured and sentenced after unfair trials following student demonstrations in 1999, continued to face violence while in custody. The brothers required medical treatment in the course of the year for their injuries. No investigations were carried out into their allegations of ill-treatment in custody. Six years after the murders of two political activists and three writers—a case known in Iran as the "Serial Murders"—no steps had been taken to bring those who ordered the killings to justice. In 1999 it had been acknowledged that the killings had been committed by state officials. During the year, former Intelligence Minister Qorbanali Dorri Nafafabadi, who had been "excused" from taking part in earlier hearings in the case, was reportedly appointed state prosecutor. Nasser Zarafshan, a human rights defender and the lawyer for the families of the two political activists, remained incarcerated following an unfair trial in 2002.

Human Rights Defenders

The award of the Nobel Peace Prize to human rights defender Shirin Ebadi in 2003 contributed to the growth and increasing self-confidence of civil society. Nevertheless, independent non-governmental organizations were hampered by a registration process that was open to undue influence. Human rights defenders also faced limitations on their movements.

Defenders of women's rights protested against discrimination against women in the justice system and in some criminal cases secured last-minute suspensions of executions or pardons.

In July, the Society for Defence of the Rights of Prisoners was granted permission to operate. The organization aimed to inform prisoners and their families of their rights and to provide material support to detainees, through training and education. However, members of the Society's Board faced politically motivated criminal charges. For example, Emaddedin Baqi was sentenced to one year's imprisonment by an appeals court in October on charges of spreading anti-state propaganda. Earlier in the month his passport had been confiscated as he prepared to leave the country to address a number of human rights conferences in North America.

Journalists and human rights defenders Mahboubeh Abbasgholizadeh and Omid Me'mariyan were arrested for a period of several weeks each on the 28th and 10th of October, respectively, possibly in connection with their Internet writings and the support they had given to independent non-governmental organizations. Tens of other civil society activists faced harassment through summons and interrogation. Those detained had "confessed" while in custody although later [they] reported to a governmental commission that these were extracted under duress.

The Legislative Response

In March, following repeated rejection, [Iran's] President [Mohammad] Khatami withdrew bills that proposed extending the powers of the President and prohibiting the Guardians' Council from disqualifying parliamentary candidates. In May, parliament again voted to ratify the UN Convention against Torture. Parliament's previous attempt to ratify the Convention had been rejected by the Guardians' Council in August 2003.

In April the Head of the Judiciary issued a judicial directive reportedly prohibiting the use of torture. In May, a little-known law concerning "respect for legitimate freedoms and preservation of civil rights" was enacted. This also contained provisions against forms of torture.

Laws giving recognized religious minorities and women more rights were enacted in 2004 but in June the incoming parliament rejected the previous parliament's passage of a bill granting women equal inheritance rights with men. In August, the Guardians' Council rejected a proposal to make Iran a state party to the UN Women's Convention.

Inhumane Punishments

At least 159 people were executed in 2004, including at least one minor. Scores of others, including at least 10 people who were under 18 at the time the crime was committed were sentenced to death. It was not known how many of these sentences had been upheld by the Supreme Court. The true figures were believed to be considerably higher. The death penalty continued to be handed down for charges such as "enmity against God" or "morality crimes" that did not reflect internationally recognizable criminal charges.

On 15 August, Atefeh Rajabi, reportedly aged 16, was hanged. She was sentenced after a grossly unfair trial during which she was publicly insulted and doubts regarding her mental state appeared to be ignored.

At least 36 people were sentenced to flogging, although the true figure was thought to be significantly higher.

Mohsen Mofidi died in February in Tehran following the imposition of a flogging sentence. No investigation was carried out by the authorities to establish whether he died as a result of the flogging.

In November and December Leyla Mafi, who was reported to be a child offender with mental disabilities, and Hajieh Esmailvand were sentenced to death, the latter reportedly by stoning. They were convicted of prostitution and other acts of immorality (*a'mal khalaf-e 'ofat*). Following domestic and international protests both women were granted a stay of execution. Afsaneh Norouzi, who was sentenced to death in 2003, had her case transferred to a conciliation council.

Torture continued to be routine in many prisons.

In July, the head of a prison in Dezful, southern Iran, was dismissed in connection with an incident in which his staff tied an inmate to a ceiling fan, severing circulation to his hands, which then had to be amputated.

> *"The Islamic Republic of Iran has spared no efforts . . . to expand its cooperation and interaction with foreign countries in the area of human rights."*

Iran Does Not Violate Human Rights

Paimaneh Hastaei

Despite the claims made by other members of the United Nations, Iran does not violate the rights of its citizens, Paimaneh Hastaei contends in this viewpoint. She asserts that criticisms of Iran by a Canadian delegation are politically motivated and disregard Iran's support of freedom of press and freedom of worship. Hastaei concludes that the Canadian efforts undermine human rights successes in Iran and hamper Iran's cooperation with other countries. Hastaei served as Iran's representative to the United Nation's human rights committee in 2003.

Editor's note: This viewpoint was originally a statement presented to the Third Committee of the United Nations (UN), a committee that focuses on social, humanitarian, and cultural issues.

Paimaneh Hastaei, "The Situation of the Human Rights in the Islamic Republic of Iran," statement before the Third Committee of the United Nations, November 30, 2003. © 2003 United Nations. Reproduced by permission.

As you read, consider the following questions:

1. Why does the author believe the sponsor of the Canadian resolution is preoccupied with issues other than human rights in Iran?

2. According to Hastaei, what do the student demonstrations in Iran indicate?

3. How many seats in Parliament are guaranteed to Iran's religious minorities, as explained by the author?

In dealing with the question before the 3rd Committee, namely the situation of the human rights in the Islamic Republic of Iran, I wish to confine myself to some brief clarifications on a number of main contentions contained in the draft resolution[1] and the introductory statement of its main sponsor.

Not About Human Rights

Allow me ... to start with a procedural point. Contrary to what was stated by Canada ..., it is unfortunate that the main sponsor of the draft resolution sought, to the extent possible, to keep my delegation in the dark as to its intention to bring this issue up in this Committee. It failed to approach us ever at the UN on this issue. We first learned of the move when the head of my delegation happened to be in Ottawa, Canada, only two weeks ago, in relation to a quite different issue, and the relevant draft was only submitted to my delegation by fax at the same time the draft was being tabled on November 17, [2003], thereby allowing no time to deliberate on the draft in informals.

Thus, we could not but conclude that the Canadian delegation, while preparing to submit its draft resolution, sought, at the same time, to deprive us from our right to prepare to

1. The resolution, which was later adopted by the committee, called for the UN General Assembly to express its concern about human rights violations in Iran and to ask Iran to make changes such as ending executions by stoning and banning torture.

present our version of the events to Member States of this Committee, enabling them to have a clear understanding of the issue.

Understandably, this unprecedented move out of the blue has taken many in this Committee by surprise. There are reasonable grounds to believe that the main sponsor of this draft resolution is chiefly preoccupied with something other than the situation of human rights in Iran. Indications in both the draft and the statement of the distinguished representative of Canada point to the fact that the Canadian delegation is acting out of discontent resulting from a point of contention in our bilateral relations. In our view, it is all the more unfortunate that a delegation seeks to turn the issue of human rights, in such an obvious way, into a means to settle scores in bilateral relations. As to the substance, allow me ... to start with the same very issue of [a] bilateral nature referred to tacitly in the draft resolution and explicitly in the Canadian statement:

The Kazemi Case

It is true that the late Zahra Kazemi, a journalist of Iranian nationality who apparently held a Canadian passport too, lost her life while she was in custody in Tehran. This occurrence was very unfortunate and saddened virtually all Iranians, be they officials or ordinary citizens. The case has ever since received a wide and ongoing coverage in the Iranian media with little precedent in the recent memory. As soon as the news broke out, the Iranian Government took every possible and necessary measure with a view to bringing all culprits to justice. The Iranian President of the Republic ordered the establishment of an inquiry committee with 4 ministers in attendance. The Iranian Parliament began its own independent investigation into the case. The relevant reports have been issued and are available in the public domain. Although charges are filed against several prison officials, and they are being tried in an open court in Tehran ... , the case is yet to be decided due to cross claims by relevant agencies.

Improvements Beyond Human Rights

The UN estimates that 94 percent of the [Iranian] population now has access to health services and safe water. The literacy rate rose from less than 50 percent in 1977 to 84 percent in 2002. Among those between six and twenty-nine years of age, it was as high as 97 percent. The infant mortality rate fell from 104 per 1,000 in the mid-1970s to 25 in 2002. Life expectancy increased from fifty-five years to sixty-nine—one of the best in the Middle East. Population growth declined from 4 percent per annum in the late 1980s to 1.2 percent in 2003—mainly due to the establishment of women's health clinics and the distribution of birth control devices.

Ervand Abrahamian, Inventing the Axis of Evil, *2004.*

It is impossible to assume that the Canadian delegation might have been ignorant of the full measures adopted by the Iranian Government in investigating the case of the late Kazemi. My Government has thus far gone to every length to exhaust cooperation [with] the Canadians on this issue. And, among other things, the Canadian ambassador to Tehran has always been personally present in the court during the hearing of the case. While we do not really understand what else they might have expected of the Iranian Government, we clearly understand why the representative of Canada failed to refer to the above facts and, instead, tried to present a distorted picture of the incident to this Committee.

At issue are not incidents or crimes that unfortunately may happen everywhere on a daily basis. What matters, especially in this Committee, is rather the way they are dealt with and the accountability of governments. It is unfortunate that in the case of the late Kazemi, the Canadian colleague focused on the occurrence and sought to keep the Committee in the dark as to the reaction to it by the Iranian Government. The same holds true in most other cases too. At the same time, it is very unfortunate that the Canadian Government has refused to extend any cooperation to my Government on a comparable case. The Canadian officials are yet to provide basic information to us on the killing by the police of an Iranian national, namely, Kaivan Tabish in Vancouver under suspicious circumstances. As the respect for human life and dignity must be universal, we expect the Canadians to be forthcoming on this issue so as to, inter alia, dissipate the suspicion of a cover-up being conducted by some Canadian agencies. . . .

Iranians Have Freedoms

The Canadian representative tried, in his statement, to infer the lack of freedom of press in Iran based on the Kazemi case. It is obvious that an isolated case cannot serve as a basis for forming a judgment on an important issue such as freedom of press in Iran. It is a well-known and established fact that the ever growing vitality in the Iranian domestic politics, especially in recent years, has given rise to [a] vibrant and energetic press. Undoubtedly, nobody claims that the Iranian press faces any difficulty; however, we can fairly assert that the Iranian Government is consistent and persistent in facilitating the publication of new and more journals.

The student demonstrations in some Iranian cities, contrary to what the Canadian statement tried to convey, were clear signs indicating the political openness and the existence of the freedom of expression in the country. In this respect, I wish to recall the tolerance on the part of the Government to the extent that even the President himself [Mohammad Khatami, at that time], in several occasion, acknowledged the right of the students to demonstrate and protest. It is also a matter of common knowledge that even the Iranian police went to a great length to protect the demonstrators against the vigilante groups who tried to assault them. The above has been the policy of the Iranian Government vis-à-vis peaceful demonstrations as opposed to violent behaviors and attempts to destruct public property. The arrests referred to in the Canadian statement meant to inhibit some attempts aimed at spreading violence and damaging public property by some elements who broke away from the orderly rally. Thus, it is unfortunate that the Canadian speaker, here too, was unfair in failing to distinguish between the violence and peaceful protest and once again distorted the fact. It is also significant to remind that my Government has always advocated and tried to facilitate the early release by courts of those arrested. And as a result, almost all the detainees were released from custody.

Likewise, it is a gross distortion of the facts to try to cast doubt on the freedom of worship and other freedoms for the religious minorities in Iran. Not only do they enjoy free gathering and worshipping in their places of choice, be they churches, synagogues or temples, arrangements are also made in the Constitution to ensure their representation in the national Parliament. As a result, Assyrians, Zoroastrians and Jews, each, elect one, and the Armenians elect two members of parliament. Other than the allocated quotas, the law does not rule out the participation of the minorities in the general elections as electors or runners for local and national office. . . .

Working with Other Countries

The Islamic Republic of Iran has spared no efforts in the past few years, especially after the non-adoption of the latest draft resolution against my country in the 57th Session of the Commission of Human Rights, to expand its cooperation and interaction with foreign countries in the area of human rights. Along the line of this policy, we established mechanisms aimed at promoting relevant dialogue with a number of countries, including the European Union [EU], Japan, Switzerland and Australia. To the extent that, in the span of one year, three rounds of dialogue with the EU were held.

The talk with the UN High-Commission for Human Rights (UNHCHR) on technical cooperations is an ongoing process. As result of an open invitation, thus far, the Working Group on Arbitrary Detention and the Special Rapporteur on the promotion and protection of the right to freedom of opinion and expression of the UNHCHR visited Iran, and both in their conclusions stressed that they encountered no restriction whatsoever in the course of fulfilling their tasks. . . .

Undermining Advancements in Human Rights

The representative of Canada, in his statement, maintained that the draft resolution before the Committee is to complement the efforts already undertaken and the achievements thus far obtained. Here, we have to reject such an assertion. There should be no doubt that the current attempt by Canada runs counter to the goal of promoting cooperation in the area of human rights and undermines the efforts already undertaken by my Government to bolster human rights achievements in Iran.

As noted earlier, we view the move by the main sponsor of the draft resolution before the Committee to be fallout of a bilateral issue and its subsequent impact on the domestic politics of the government concerned. Moreover, the draft is intrusive and seeks to interfere in the Iranian domestic affairs. For instance, the call upon the Iranian Government to appoint an impartial prosecutor is just an example in this respect.

Allow me . . . to conclude by asserting that the draft resolution before this Committee is counterproductive and discourages the ongoing approach based on the promotion of cooperation between Iran and the international community on human rights. The hidden as well as selfish agenda behind this draft contradicts the purpose of those countries that genuinely seek to promote human rights at the international level.

Therefore, I wish to close by appealing to the distinguished delegates to extend their support to the ongoing process of promotion of human rights in Iran by voting against the draft resolution under consideration.

"The feminist movement in Iran is very strong at this time and we will succeed in changing the laws."

Women's Rights Are Improving in Iran

Shirin Ebadi, interviewed by Jacqueline M. Massey

In the following viewpoint Shirin Ebadi contends that Iranian women have achieved several successes, including reforms of custody laws and a growing presence in the nation's universities. She also claims that more women today believe in equality of the sexes. Ebadi acknowledges, however, that Iran's women continue to face oppression, particularly in regard to their rights under family law. Ebadi is an Iranian human rights attorney who won the Nobel Peace Prize in 2003. Jacqueline M. Massey is a freelance writer.

As you read, consider the following questions:

1. According to Ebadi, what was the only example of Iran's president supporting women's rights?

2. What percentage of Iran's university population is female?

Shirin Ebadi, interviewed by Jacqueline M. Massey, "A Nobel Cause: Shirin Ebadi Leads the Charge for Human Rights in Iran," *Herizons*, vol. 18, no. 2, Fall 2004, p. 16. © 2004 Jacqueline M. Massey. Reproduced by permission.

3. What issue does Ebadi consider to be most important?

When she won the Nobel Peace Prize in 2003, Shirin Ebadi became the first Iranian, the 11th woman and the third Muslim to receive the honour. Ebadi had been Iran's first female judge, a position she lost after the 1979 Iranian Revolution when the mullahs who assumed power deemed women too weak-minded for the job.

Now 56, Ebadi is a civil rights activist and human rights defence attorney in a country where women's legal worth is only half that of men's. A mother of two, Ebadi has written numerous books and founded the Society for the Protection of the Rights of the Child. She continues to lecture at the University of Tehran, believing that women's education is the key to overcoming a culture that has limited their rights.

Ebadi's Beliefs

While Ebadi remains fierce in her condemnation of Iranian laws that are a blow against the rights and freedoms of women, she is equally critical of other countries such as the United States. She continues despite the fact that her outspokenness has endangered her life—Ebadi has survived two assassination attempts and was imprisoned in Iran for "disturbing public opinion."

While accepting the peace prize in Oslo, Ebadi said, "The discriminatory plight of women in Islamic states has its roots in the patriarchal and male-dominated culture prevailing in these societies, not in Islam. This culture does not tolerate freedom and democracy, just as it does not believe in the equal rights of men and women. . . . The liberation of women . . . would threaten the historical and traditional position of the rulers and guardians of that culture."

Ebadi has taken on politically explosive cases, earning the ire of conservatives and the hatred of fundamentalists in Iran. She acted on behalf of the families of writers and intellectuals killed in the late 1990s, and she continues to demand the release of political prisoners and journalists. More recently, Ebadi has taken on the case of slain photojournalist Zahra Kazemi, who died after being taken into custody in Iran in 2003. Ebadi's high-profile involvement in the case guarantees that the circumstances surrounding the Canadian woman's death will not quietly disappear into the corridors of diplomatic channels. She has vowed to take the case to "international systems and communities."

In this *Herizons* interview, Ebadi spoke in Farsi and her words were translated by Professor Ahmad Karimi-Hakkak.

The Nobel Prize and Its Aftermath

Herizons: How has winning the Nobel Peace Prize affected your struggle for human rights in Iran?

Shirin Ebadi: It has made more work for me! More meetings, more travel. More interviews. And what this means is that my voice can be heard louder and clearer and I am very happy and grateful for this.

Some of your critics, especially those living outside their Iranian homeland, have said they were disappointed that you have not taken a harder line against conservative clerics and other Muslim leaders who say they are following the Qur'an and upholding Shari'a law in espousing dictates that suppress the rights and freedoms of women. They question why you do not advocate the separation of religion and state. What would your response be to these critics, and how compatible are human rights with Islam?

Look, when an event occurs or a talk is given, not everyone interprets it the same way.

It's very natural that various opinions may exist about me. I have respect for the opinions that are opposite to mine. But I firmly believe that what has caused the backwardness in Iran for women is erroneous interpretations of Islam.

As an example, when we protest and say, 'Why should men be allowed to take four wives?' they say, 'Because this is the dictate of Islam.' So the answer would have to come out from the heart of Islam. And we should prove that Islam can be interpreted in another way.

Challenging Discrimination

So how do you challenge the hard-line elements who control Iran, who misuse and abuse their power, who interpret the Qur'an in such a way that sustains discrimination and ensures that women are disenfranchised?

The way we have done it before. One would have to respond to any opinion on the basis of reason. In order to develop a reasoning process one would have to write books and articles and speak at various forums. I have written 11 books in Iran and published extensively. Every month I have a few articles. Wherever and whenever I have an opportunity to speak to people, I seize it.

The current president of Iran, Mohammad Khatami,[1] rose to his position largely because of the support of women who hoped he could bring some relief to their plight in Iran. What do you think of his record, and do you have much confidence in his ability to advocate for women's rights?

It's true that Khatami would never have been elected without widespread support from women. Women expected much from Khatami and they were hopeful that he would submit various bills to the parliament in support of women's rights. But the only thing he presented to the parliament was for Iran to join the [United Nations] Convention on the Eradication of All Forms of Discrimination Against Women.

The Majlis [Iran's parliament] ratified this bill but the Guardian Council [a constitutional body of the upper parliament] opposed it.

1. Khatami's second term as president ended in 2005. He was succeeded by Mahmoud Ahmadinejad.

Progress Throughout the Middle East

Courageous women such as Shirin Ebadi have made women prime movers in the struggle for a more liberal democratic order, and the status of women is now a key barometer of progress. In Jordan, women launched a campaign against so-called "honor killings," in which men kill female relatives who bring "dishonor" on the family. In Kuwait, women who participated in the resistance to the Iraqi occupation of 1990–91 started a campaign for women's suffrage after the Iraqis were driven out. In Iran, women successfully campaigned against the stoning and flogging of their sisters. In Saudi Arabia, a brave group publicly challenged the authorities in 1990 by the simple but bold step of driving their own cars.

Haleh Esfandiari, Wilson Quarterly, *Spring 2004.*

I personally expected Mr. Khatami to present more bills, even though I knew that the Guardian Council would oppose them all.

The Culture of Patriarchy

In terms of laws that discriminate against women you have said, "Islam is not the problem. It is the culture of patriarchy." So how do you go about breaking through that culture of patriarchy?

To struggle against the patriarchal culture one would have to know it very well. And then we have to start struggling against it on the basis of education, especially at the level of women's education. And let me add that patriarchal culture is not simply against women. It also doesn't accept the principles of democracy. This is a tribal culture that puts one person on the pedestal to act and speak on behalf of all.

Can you name one country where women's situation is good but there is no democracy?

No. And I know because I have studied these countries one by one. Yet in Canada, even though we can celebrate having a democratic country, patriarchal culture still exists.

Patriarchal culture is very weak here [in Canada], and to the extent that it is weak democracy has gained strength. Women's conditions for you are good, at least in the law. And to the extent that women's condition is good in law, democracy is good in law as well.

Signs of Improvement

I have read that more and more women are being accepted into universities in Iran. Do you see this as a strong sign in terms of educating women about the culture of patriarchy?

Absolutely. At the beginning of the Revolution [in 1979], the maximum percentage of women in the universities was 25 percent. And what we argued in favour of feminism was protested against even by women themselves. But I am pleased to see that, 24 years later, 63 percent of our university population is female.

Many of the things that we used to say then, and that women objected to, now women say and go beyond. And I am happy to report that, at this time, both the elite women and the common womenfolk seem to be forming a single stance. The feminist movement in Iran is very strong at this time and we will succeed in changing the laws.

[In 2004,] we were able to change the custody laws. It was a great victory for women. And we will have victories like this in the future. But that does not mean that the state, the government, is going to hand it to us on a plate.

What I mean to say is that this feminist movement is so strong that we can grab it from the government.

You have called for a legal review of issues related to the civil rights of women, including such subjects as family law, the quality of couples' rights, the legal relations of mother and child, punitive laws like blood money, and issues resulting from unemployment. Has there been significant progress in any of these areas? What gains have been made?

We have all of these problems. And that's why I say that the women's legal situation in Iran is unsuitable. And that's why the feminist movement has increased so much in strength. If the women in a society felt themselves on an equal footing, there would be no reason for a feminist movement.

What I want to emphasize is that at the beginning of the Revolution, when we expressed opinions like this, only a very select few women agreed with us. But now this agreement has spread all over the place.

Family Law Must Be Changed

What is the most important issue that needs addressing at the present time?

The most important thing is the change in family laws. Because family laws embrace all women, we have to change quite a few things.

For instance, polygamy will have to go. According to Iranian laws at the present time, a man can divorce his wife at any time presenting no reasons at all. But a woman can file for divorce on only very specific and limited grounds. Common property—the mutuality of ownership—does not exist. It has been specified in law that the man is head of the household. When a woman applies for a passport she has to present her husband's consent. But a man can travel without even informing his wife.

Are you optimistic about the future of your country in terms of the situation concerning human rights?

We think one would have to be hopeful and optimistic all the time and for all reasons. Because the day when I cease to be hopeful and optimistic [is the day] I can't work any longer.

Because of your outspoken stand for human rights and your work as a lawyer and activist, you have been forced to withstand verbal abuse, censorship and even imprisonment. Your life has been threatened, and I'm sure your family worries about you a great deal. What has been the hardest aspect of living the life you have chosen as a spokesperson and activist for the oppressed?

Activists for human rights all over the world have to face threats. This is the kind of life I have chosen for myself. So what you call the hard aspect is easy for me to bear because it has been my choice. When an athlete who wants to win a game gets up early and does what it takes, he doesn't think of it as hardship.

We may think that athlete's life is very difficult, but it's his choice and so it's easy for him. That's what my life is for me.

Do Not Transmit Patriarchy

You have worked tirelessly as a judge, a lawyer and a human rights activist. You are an author and a teacher. At this time in your life, what do you see as your most important role?

If I were to introduce myself, I would put all those things together and call myself an attorney who works for human rights.

Do you have a message for women everywhere who are oppressed and burdened under the cloak of patriarchy?

My message is this—that women, at the same time they are victims of this culture, are carriers of this culture. I liken this culture to hemophilia as a disease, which women do not catch but carry and give to their sons. Let's not forget that any patriarchal man has been raised in the lap of women. So women must pay particular attention to not becoming carriers of this culture.

> *"There is no compatibility between Islam and democracy, equality and justice for all."*

Women's Rights Are Not Improving in Iran

Parvin Darabi

In the following viewpoint Parvin Darabi asserts that women's rights do not exist in Islamic nations such as Iran. According to Darabi, women have been oppressed and silenced by a regime that adheres to the Islamic belief that women should always be subservient to men. Darabi concludes that the only way to stop the mistreatment of Iranian women is by fighting for the end of theocracies. Darabi is the founder of the Dr. Homa Darabi Foundation, a U.S.–based organization that promotes the rights of women and children.

As you read, consider the following questions:

1. What was Darabi's objective when she began to research Islam?

2. Why does Darabi doubt the truth of Mohammed's revelations?

Parvin Darabi, "Islam and Oppression of Women," speech at the Jerusalem Summit, http://forum.homa.org/index.php?showtopic=20. Dr. Homa Darabi Foundation, November 28, 2004. Reproduced by permission.

3. According to the author, why did Zahra Kazemi die?

"We have just enough religion to make us hate, and not enough to love one another!"

—*Jonathan Swift, 18th-century writer and philosopher*

On February 21, 1994 I was a very happy-going successful engineering consultant. I thought I had it all, money, stature, a nice home, supportive husband, an adorable son, and a fulfilling profession. Then on February 22 came the early morning phone call from my uncle in Tehran, which shattered my world and changed the direction of my life forever. On that early morning I learned about my sister Homa's self-immolation protest in a public square in Tehran against the oppressive regime of the Islamic Republic of Iran and their treatment of women. Her last cries were, "Death to tyranny, long live freedom, long live Iran."

A Well-Respected Doctor

My sister, Homa, in addition to being a doctor of medicine, was an outspoken feminist and a political activist. In 1990 she was ordered to comply with the strict rules of hijab, the covering of women. She refused.

With her refusal, she became the target of an ordeal uncounted women of all ages are facing in the Islamic societies today and throughout the history of Islam.

Homa was a medical doctor, who specialized in Pediatrics, General Psychiatry and Child and Adolescent Psychiatry and was licensed to practice medicine in 49 states of the United States (except Florida).

To help Iranian children suffering from mental disorders, who were denied care and often ignored, she returned to Iran in 1976 and was hired as a professor at the University of Tehran School of Medicine. She opened her private practice at the same time and very quickly became known throughout Iran for her advanced approach to mental health.

She established the first children's psychiatric clinic in Tehran.

Kjell Nilsson-Maki. Reproduced by permission.

Silencing an Outspoken Woman

During the 1978 revolution, she was one of the strong supporters of Iran's democratic revolution; however, when democracy was hijacked by Islamic theocracy, Homa became devastated and totally broke away from all politics. She then devoted her time to her profession as a medical doctor and continued her struggles as a women's rights activist.

In 1992, at a medical conference in Tehran she stated that without a chador (the cover for Iranian women) a woman couldn't do much; however under the chador she could do everything, including carrying guns and bombs.

To silence her, in retaliation, she was first fired from her position as a professor of Medicine at the University of Tehran and was later harassed in her private practice. At age 54, she finally had to close down her practice, and be confined to her home for the first time in her life.

As a prominent psychiatrist, her services were requested by devastated and helpless parents whose daughters were subjected to flogging and beating for such violations as wearing make-up and nylons. These devastated parents would beg her to go to the courts and declare their daughters insane to suspend their punishment.

To label a perfectly, healthy, sane young woman insane was not an issue with those desperate parents. They wanted their daughters unharmed, but it was an agonizing issue with Homa. She was ruining a young life forever. The book *Rage Against the Veil* written by my son and myself [and] published in English by Prometheus Books, describes the courageous life and death of my sister, Homa. The book has been published in German, Dutch and Persian.

Not Compatible with Equality

Following the loss of my sister I could no longer continue with my profession. Someone had to speak on behalf of millions of oppressed women living under the Islamic laws of Sharia.[1] I established [the] Dr. Homa Darabi Foundation, a nonprofit organization concerned with all violations of human rights focusing on defending the rights of women against religious, cultural and social abuse.

I felt compelled to act, so I began my research in Islam. My objective was to gain knowledge about a religion or implementation of the rules and laws of that religion, which makes a healthy, educated, accomplished and life-loving physician, a mother, wife, daughter and sister with so much to look forward to, to take her own life publicly in such horrific manner, as protest against oppression of women in the Islamic Republic of Iran.

1. Islamic laws based on the Koran and the practices of Mohammed.

Growing up in Tehran in a family of by-name-only Muslims, we had very little religious education. Religion was not an issue in our family. My sister and I watched our parents at different times perform some of the religious rituals such as sacrificing a lamb, making charitable contributions and so on. In reality many of those rituals were fundamentally Persian traditions.

After 10 years of researching Islam I have come to the conclusion that there is no compatibility between Islam and democracy, equality and justice for all. . . .

Subservience Is Illogical

Islam has always spread by striking terror in the hearts of the people. By promising men superiority above women, by requiring total submission to Allah as interpreted by the clergy, by assuring them of wine and virgins in heaven and four permanent wives and as many as they want as slaves or concubines and by casting terror in the minds of nonbelievers.

We must realize that the Prophet Mohammed suffered from epilepsy. His revelations have been recited by him following his seizures. And indeed the revelations were collected and published in the latter part of the 7th century decades after his death.

Today we are living in the 21st century. Secular democracies have enabled us to succeed in science and technology. We live much longer and are more prosperous. It is not logical to ask women to be subservient to the will of their fathers, husbands and/or sons or grandsons.

It is not comprehensible to mandate that all women must stay home, bear children, submit to the will of their providers and accept to be one of the four co-wives.

Women Should Be Equal to Men

Women have proven time and time again that they are capable of performing any task from leading their nations in times of peace and prosperity to war and destruction just as well as men. Is it acceptable to ask half the world's population to live as slaves to their male counterparts?

Should women's lives in the 21st century be worth only half that of a man, any man? Should their testimony in the court of law be not accepted as fully as that of a man? Should women be stoned to death in this century because of adultery? Should nine-year-old girls be given away in marriage to men old enough to be their grandfather, or any man regardless of their age?

A 9-year-old girl is not a woman. She is just a child and climate has nothing to do with it. A 9-year-old in the hot deserts of Saudi Arabia is the same as a 9-year-old in glaciers of Alaska or mild temperatures in Madrid.

Should women be forbidden to apply for divorce, get custody of their children, strive for a better life by going to universities and studying any subject that they please? Shouldn't all women from every country around the globe be able to compete at the international Olympics forum? Should anyone be killed for criticizing any religion, including Islam? Like they did to [Theo] Van Gogh in the Netherlands for making a documentary critical of Islam?

Abuses in Iran

Millions of men, women and children have been tortured, flogged, burned, stoned to death and left alone in dungeons in our history due to religious tyranny.

Today, in the Islamic Republic of Iran, women such as Mahboubeh Abbasgholizadeh, and Fereshteh Ghazi, two Iranian journalists and human rights activists have been detained in solitary confinement for 'acts against national security and spreading propaganda.'

Should such women as Zahra Kazemi, an Iranian-Canadian journalist, die under Islamic torture apparatus for just taking pictures of the parents of the detainees outside the infamous Evin Prison in Tehran?

Or should an educated medical doctor such as my sister Dr. Homa Darabi be removed from her position because she did not cover properly? Or a fourteen-year-old should be flogged to death as it was done in Iran for eating in public during Ramadan just a couple of weeks ago?

Theocracies Must End

It is a crime for the world to stay silent against these atrocities done to men, women and children in the name of some religious edict given centuries ago.

Human beings have traveled from ice age to the stone age to the agricultural age, to industrial age and today, we live in the information age. However, it is with great regret to report that the religious dogma is still alive and trying with enormous force to take us back to the dark ages.

The Sharia laws must be discarded in order to establish secular democracies. Madrasas [Islamic schools] where boys are taken from their home and parents at age five to sit and memorize the revelations in Arabic without comprehension until they reach the age 15 must be closed. Instead we must build secular preschools, schools, and universities with scientific curricula for our children and grandchildren to strive and succeed in a peaceful world.

If we could add the number of people who have lost their lives due to religious dogma that number would exceed the collective number of people who died in wars throughout the history of mankind.

The only way to stop the religiously based terrorism is for the freedom-loving people of the world to join us to fight for secular democracies and an end to all theocracies. We, at Dr. Homa Darabi Foundation, are not alone. There are many organizations and individuals who are working hard to end the religious terrorism through education and understanding.

[In November 2004] as many as 20,000 took to the streets in the western German City of Cologne to protest the use of violence in the name of Islam with [the] slogan "Hand in Hand for Peace and Against Terror." Chancellor Gerhard Schroeder called on Muslims living in Germany to better integrate themselves into German society and warned against what he called a "conflict of cultures".

We must join them.

"The state has a monopoly on public discourse, and intellectuals . . . are simply not heard."

Censorship Is Commonplace in Iran

Farouz Farzami

Censorship of journalists and intellectuals occurs regularly in Iran, Farouz Farzami asserts in the following viewpoint. Farzami contends that because the state controls public discourse, criticisms of the government are not heard. The author further argues that state censorship has discouraged Iran's writers and journalists from being politically active. Farzami is an Iranian journalist.

As you read, consider the following questions:

1. Why does the author believe learning has become irrelevant in Iran?

2. How many Iranian newspapers and periodicals have been shut down since April 2000, according to Farzami?

3. What does Issa Saharkhiz, as cited by Farzami, urge journalists to do?

When Friday Prayer here [Tehran, Iran] finishes at about two o'clock in the afternoon, hundreds of worshipers parade toward waiting buses east of Tehran University, shouting canned rhetoric against America and Israel, defining themselves by their animosity toward others. Watching this ritual, one cannot help but ask a soul-searching question: "How can such a small minority of vocal people—totally orchestrated worshipers and their security guards—set the agenda for a nation of 70 million people?"

Intellectuals Are Silenced

The short answer is lack of free speech—or, more accurately, the absence of freedom *after* speech. The state has a monopoly on public discourse, and intellectuals, whether they are religious, atheist or agnostic, are simply not heard. The mullahs in Qom, the holy city two hours drive southwest of Tehran, can dial the phone number of any revolutionary judge in Iran and order the persecution of anyone who dares to question the authorities and their divine agenda.

Learning is thus made irrelevant. The educated must rely on the government to earn their living. I have dozens of friends who hate the religious regime but, to earn a subsistence salary, work as translators of confidential bulletins that keep the ruling theocracy abreast of what the "unfriendly" foreign news media think about Iran. "It is like preparing your own cross for your own crucifixion," said a friend who works for Iranian Radio & TV, which is controlled by the country's supreme leader, Ayatollah Ali Khamenei.

His remark reminds me of when I worked in a wood-pulp mill in western Iran during the early years of the Islamic revolution. In the first decade after 1979, many intellectuals, anticipating being arrested, cleared their bookshelves and left their "illegal" volumes on street corners. Piles of these books found their way to the mill, where we reduced them to pulp. One day, throwing books into the mill, I grasped a Farsi ver-

Internet Censorship in Iran

[Iran's government] has blocked thousands of Web sites, including—contrary to its claims that it welcomes criticism—sites that criticize government policies or report stories the government does not wish to see published. It has sought to limit the spread of blogs by blocking popular Web sites that offer free publishing tools for blogs.

Iran has the potential to become a world leader in information technology. It has a young, educated, computer-literate population that has quickly taken to the Internet. It is rapidly developing its telecommunications infrastructure. Attempts to restrict Internet usage violate Iran's obligation to protect freedom of expression and foster popular mistrust of the government.

Human Rights Watch, False Freedom, *2004.*

sion of Marx's "Capital." Immediately, I knew it was my own copy; I recognized the book by its feel, it was so familiar to my touch.

Today's intellectuals, if they haven't turned to smoking opium or drinking homemade liquor, devote themselves to literature, primarily Farsi, European, Russian and South American. The few who remain politically active, mostly defeated reformists, take refuge in religion and fast for a day, half-seriously dubbing it a "hunger strike" or "political fasting."

Protests Are Rare

There have been a few notable exceptions. [In the summer of 2004,] hundreds of staff writers from a banned daily newspaper, *Vaghayeh Etefaghieh,* protested in public, with their hands tied together as a symbol of state repression. The act drew the attention of international photojournalists, and the protest picked up steam. Soon, Iran's Nobel Peace Prize winner, Shirin Ebadi, flanked by her co-workers from the Human Rights Defendant Center, appeared at the small auditorium of the Iranian Journalists Association to throw their weight behind the protest.

Such moments, however, are rare. Since April 2000, some 110 dailies and periodicals have been closed by the authorities. Although the reform-minded Ministry of Culture and Islamic Guidance still gives moral and financial support to the managers and license-holders of the press, most independent reporters—including myself—are now barred from writing.

Taking an Active Approach

I know at least 10 journalists, public supporters of the reforms advocated by [former] President Mohammad Khatami, who have sought asylum in Europe. I sympathize with this resigned approach, but am encouraged by the more determined newcomers. The chairman of the Iranian Press Managers Board, Issa Saharkhiz, has urged journalists to protest more actively, saying: "Enough is enough. What are you waiting for? What worse can happen to you?"

He criticized those reporters who practice self-censorship, trading away their freedom of expression in hopes that their publications will survive the government crackdown. He called for journalists to end the "vicious circle of getting permission to publish and after a while being closed down."

Mr. Saharkhiz also says that jailed journalists are forced to write detailed information about their colleagues' private lives, which can be used against them whenever the judiciary branch chooses. When jailed journalists are bailed out or released, their interrogators debrief them regularly, coercing them into becoming spies for the regime.

Such is the lot of not just journalists but also writers, artists, scholars and millions of frustrated youths in Iran. Until a real political leadership rises from the ashes of the revolution, we may have to be content with it.

The vast majority of people here cross their fingers for a sudden explosion, or pray for American successes in Iraq and Afghanistan to increase the price of suppression by the theocracy in Iran. But that is the limit. Just as minimalism is the fashion in short-story writing today, I suppose we must accept minimalist politics as well.

| "Homosexual acts have been considered a capital crime in Iran since the 1979 revolution."

Iran Brutalizes Homosexuals

Doug Ireland

In the following viewpoint Doug Ireland contends that life for gay Iranians is dangerous. According to Ireland, Iranians found guilty of committing homosexual acts face torture and execution. They are also forced to report the names of other gays, who are subsequently rounded up by authorities, he claims. Ireland is a contributing editor for In These Times *and a journalist whose work has appeared in the* Village Voice, *the* Nation, *and* Vanity Fair.

As you read, consider the following questions:

1. According to Ireland, why were the hangings of two homosexual teenagers in Iran illegal?
2. Why was Amir first arrested, as explained by the author?
3. What comparison does Ireland make between the reactions of American and European gay rights organizations?

Doug Ireland, "Iran's Anti-Gay Pogrom," *In These Times*, vol. 30, no. 1, January 2006. © 2006 In These Times. Reproduced by permission of the publisher, www.intheseti mes.com.

The Islamic Republic of Iran—under the new government of President Mahmoud Ahmadinejad—is engaged in a major anti-homosexual pogrom targeting gays and gay sex. This campaign includes Internet entrapment, blackmail to force arrested gays to inform on others, torture and executions of those found guilty of engaging in "homosexual acts." Homosexual acts have been considered a capital crime in Iran since the 1979 revolution that brought the Ayatollah [Ruholla] Khomeini to power. Iranians found guilty of gay lovemaking are given a choice of four death styles: being hanged, stoned, halved by a sword or dropped from the highest perch. According to Article 152 of Iran's penal law, if two men not related by blood are found naked under one cover without good reason, both will be punished at a judge's discretion.

Executing Gay Teenagers

Iran's crackdown on gays drew worldwide protests (except in the United States) after the hanging for "homosexual acts" of two teenagers—one 18, the other believed to be 16 or 17—on July 19 [2005] in the city of Mashad. Charges against the two teens included the alleged rape of another youth. But three independent gay sources inside Mashad told Afdhere Jaffa, editor of Huriyah (an Internet 'zine for gay Muslims), that the teens were well known in the city's underground gay community as lovers who lived together, and that the rape charge was fabricated. The editors of an underground Persian-language 'zine in Iran (who requested anonymity out of fear) also confirm that their own Mashad sources said that the rape charge was trumped up—a view now generally accepted. In any case, the hangings were illegal under international law because Iran is a signatory to two treaties that forbid executing minors. Since then, there have been reports of at least a dozen more gay victims who have been executed.

"Under Islamic law, which has been adopted by Iran's legal system, it takes four witnesses to prove an act of homosexual-

Making Excuses

When it comes to the oppression of gays and lesbians in Muslim countries, gay activism hasn't died; it never really existed. Gay activists have used two types of excuses to justify their failure to aggressively mobilize for the rights of gay Muslims—moral and strategic. The moral argument is that Americans are in no position to criticize Iranians on human rights—that it would be wrong to campaign too loudly against Iranian abuses when the United States has so many problems of its own. . . .

It is the moral argument that is particularly troubling, because it suggests that some gay and lesbian leaders feel more allegiance to the relativism of the contemporary left than they do to the universality of their own cause.

Rob Anderson, New Republic Online, *October 6, 2005. www.tnr.com.*

ity, which is a capital crime. That's why it's much easier for the Islamic government to invent other criminal charges against gay people to get rid of them," Jama told me. The Iranian gay 'zine's editors said the same, urging Westerners to be "very careful" before accepting such criminal charges at face value, as they are "most likely false."

One Man's Experience

Amir is a 22-year-old gay Iranian who was arrested by Iran's religious morality police as part of a massive Internet entrapment campaign targeting gays. He escaped from Iran in August [2005], and is now in Turkey seeking asylum in a gay-friendly country. Through a Persian translator, Amir gave me a terrifying, firsthand account of the anti-gay crackdown. Amir's first arrest for being gay came when police raided a private party. "The judge told me, 'If we send you to a physician who vouches that your rectum has been penetrated in any way, you will be sentenced to death," says Amir. He was fined and released for lack of proof that a sexual act had taken place.

Later, an unrepentant Amir set up a meeting with a man he met through a Yahoo! gay chat room. When his date turned out to be a member of the sex police, Amir was arrested and taken to Intelligence Ministry headquarters, "a very scary place," he says. "There I denied that I was gay—but they showed me a printout from the chat room of my messages and my pictures." Then, says Amir, the torture began. "There was a metal chair in the middle of the room—they put a gas flame under the chair and made me sit on it as the metal seat got hotter and hotter. They threatened to send me to an army barracks where all the soldiers were going to rape me. The leader told one of the other officers to take [a soft drink] bottle and shove it up my ass, screaming, 'This will teach you not to want any more cock!' I was so afraid of sitting in that metal chair as it got hotter and hotter that I confessed. Then they brought out my file and told me that I was a 'famous faggot' in Shiraz. They beat me up so badly that I passed out and was thrown, unconscious, into a holding cell.

"When I came to, I saw there were several dozen other gay guys in the cell with me. One of them told me that after they had taken him in, they beat him and forced him to set up dates with people through chat rooms—and each one of those people had been arrested; those were the other people in that cell with me."

Eventually tried, Amir was sentenced to 100 lashes. "I passed out before the 100 lashes were over. When I woke up, my arms and legs were so numb that I fell over when they picked me up from the platform on which I'd been lashed. They had told me that if I screamed, they would beat me even harder—so I was biting my arms so hard, to keep from screaming, that I left deep teeth wounds in my own arms."

Americans Are Not Responding

After this entrapment and public flogging, Amir's life became unbearable. He was rousted regularly at his home by the *basiji* (a para-police made up of thugs recruited from the criminal classes and the ... unemployed) and by agents of the Office for Promotion of Virtue and Prohibition of Vice, which re-presses "moral deviance"—things like boys and girls walking around holding hands, women not wearing proper Islamic dress and prostitution. Says Amir, "In one of these arrests, Colonel Javanmardi told me that if they catch me again that I would be put to death, 'just like the boys in Mashad.' He said it just like that, very simply, very explicitly. He didn't mince words. We all know that the boys who were hanged in Mashad were gay—the rape charges against them were trumped up, just like the charges of theft and kidnapping against them. When you get arrested, you are forced by beatings, torture and threats to confess to crimes you didn't commit. It happens all the time, and has to friends of mine."

Amir's experience is typical—as is the lack of concern evi-denced by U.S. LGBT [lesbian/gay/bisexual/transgender] orga-nizations. Both of the principal U.S. gay rights organizations—Human Rights Campaign and the National Gay and Lesbian Task Force—have failed to incorporate international solidarity with persecuted gays into their fundraising-driven agendas, and neither have mobilized public protests against Iran's anti-gay pogrom. Their European counterparts, in contrast, orga-nized multiple demonstrations at Iranian embassies across the Continent.

The Persian Gay and Lesbian Organization (PGLO) is the principal group for Iranian gays, claiming 29,000 on its e-mail list. The PGLO—which publishes a monthly Internet maga-zine in Persian, hosts radio netcasts into Iran, and has secre-tariats in Turkey and Norway—has appealed to Western gays to mobilize international protests against the inhumane trag-edy that has befallen Iranian same-sexers.

Periodical Bibliography

The following articles have been selected to supplement the diverse views presented in this chapter.

Mariah Blake   "Targeting Tehran," *Columbia Journalism Review*, November/December 2004.

Haleh Esfandiari   "Iranian Women, Please Stand Up," *Foreign Policy*, November/December 2005.

Haleh Esfandiari   "The Woman Question," *Wilson Quarterly*, Spring 2004.

Nazila Fathi   "Taboo Surfing," *New York Times*, August 4, 2002.

Scott Macleod   "One Woman's Way," *Time International*, December 15, 2003.

Chris Richards   "Interview with the Association of Iranian Blogwriters," *New Internationalist*, May 2005.

Ramesh Sepehrrad and Donna M. Hughes   "Iran: Sex Slavery New Face of Oppression of Women in Iran," *Women's eNews*, February 1, 2004. www.womensenews.org

Jay Tolson   "Faith & Freedom," *U.S. News & World Report*, November 10, 2003.

Milan Vesely   "www.irantopsites.com," *Middle East*, November 2004.

CHAPTER 3

How Should the United States Respond to Iran?

Chapter Preface

The attitude that the United States has toward Iran cannot be described as exclusively positive or negative. While the U.S. government may want to make use of Iran both as a source of oil and as an influential player in Middle East politics, many aspects of Iran, such as its hard-line Islamic regime and its nuclear ambitions, have prompted concerns. Iran's research into nuclear weapons, particularly, has sparked fervent debate as to whether the United States should take military action against that nation. If it does, it would be the first war between the two countries, but it would not be the first time the U.S. government has been involved militarily in Iran's affairs. During the eight-year-long Iran-Iraq War (1980–1988), the United States worked both for and against Iran.

The war began in September 1980, after Iraq invaded Iran. It was not surprising that the United States initially supported Iraq in the conflict. At the time of the invasion, fifty-two American hostages were being held by Iranian revolutionaries in the U.S. embassy in Tehran (they were not released until January 1981, after 444 days of captivity). The hostage-taking had occurred following the overthrow of Muhammad Reza Shah Pahlavi, the ruler of Iran and a U.S. ally. Upon learning that the shah was receiving medical treatment in the United States, five hundred Iranians seized the embassy. Concern over the hostages was not the only reason America sided with Iraq, however. As journalist Michael Dobbs explains in a *Washington Post* article, the United States was concerned about the oil supply when determining which nation to support: "After its initial gains, Iraq was on the defensive, and Iranian troops had advanced to within a few miles of Basra, Iraq's second largest city. U.S. intelligence information suggested the Iranians might achieve a breakthrough on the Basra front, destabilizing Kuwait, the Gulf states, and even Saudi Arabia, thereby threatening U.S. oil supplies."

Toward the end of the Iran-Iraq War, the United States altered its position, and its sudden support of Iran became a political scandal. Members of the Ronald Reagan administration secretly sold arms to Iran and used the funds to provide financial support to the Contra rebels in Nicaragua, who were trying to overthrow the incumbent Sandinista regime. These actions circumvented rules passed by Congress that prohibited the provision of aid to the Contras and led to investigations in 1986 and 1987. Larry Everest, writing for the Web site ZNet, contends that the U.S. government was cynical in its response to the Iran-Iraq War: "During the Iran-Iraq War, the U.S. cynically tilted to one side, then the other." The war ended with a cease-fire in August 1988.

The contradictory attitudes toward Iran held by the United States in the 1980s remain present today. While the U.S. government considers the possibility of war with Iran, it also must evaluate whether to work with Iranians in order to help that nation become more democratic. In the following chapter the authors debate how the United States should best respond to the political and military situations in Iran.

| *"Air strikes on their nuclear weapons surface sites won't stop the program, but can slow Iran's progress for months or years."* |

The United States Must Use Military Strikes to End Iran's Nuclear Weapons Program

Jed Babbin

In the following viewpoint Jed Babbin contends that Iran is a dangerous nation whose efforts to build nuclear weapons present a threat that can only be prevented through U.S. military intervention. According to Babbin, Iran supports terrorism and wants to use nuclear weapons to further aid the terrorist organization al Qaeda. Babbin argues that American air strikes on Iran's nuclear weapons surface sites is the only viable way to slow that nation's nuclear research. Babbin is a contributing editor for American Spectator.

As you read, consider the following questions:

1. What must occur before America can withdraw from Iraq, in Babbin's view?

Jed Babbin, "Exit Strategies," *American Spectator*, February 2005, pp. 18–21. Copyright © 2005 The American Spectator. Reproduced by permission.

2. Why does the author believe it is an understatement to call Iran a terrorist nation?

3. According to Babbin, why is Mujahideen e-Khalq (MEK) on America's list of foreign terror organizations?

To deal with terrorism we have to destroy its sources. Those sources have little or nothing to do with poverty or public relations. The sources of terrorism are the jihadist ideology[1] and the nations that base their imperial ambitions on its success. Were we to identify those sources clearly, and define the means of defeating them, we would have a clear vision of what winning requires. To begin to do that, we have to speak loudly those thoughts that have only occasionally been whispered.

Destroying Jihadist Ideology

The first of those thoughts is that no matter the result of the Iraqi election America cannot withdraw from Iraq until the remaining terrorist regimes in the region are neutralized. That unpalatable fact results from two facts, that the jihadist regimes of Iran, Syria, and Saudi Arabia cannot leave a democratic Iraq at peace and that those regimes are jihadist themselves and large sources of terrorism.

The second is that military action will be necessary, in one degree or another, to destroy the other sources of jihadism. That we are building a number of military bases in Iraq is, to the U.N. [United Nations], Old Europe, and the Democrats, an unnecessary provocation of the terrorists. Heaven forbid that we would offend those who hack off the heads of helpless Americans and other hostages. The terrorists may well derive some propaganda benefit from our presence, but the military advantage we gain outweighs that by—in strategic airlift

1. *Jihad* means "holy war." Some Muslims believe that they are bound by their religion to engage in holy war to defeat the infidels (non-Muslims), including the United States and its allies.

terms—millions of ton-miles per day. We don't have to "get there fustest with the mostest." We're already there, and can get on with the job of destroying jihadist ideology and supporters. . . .

To defeat the jihadist ideology, we have to fight it as we did the Soviets'. There should be a continuous stream of American information being broadcast into the Muslim nations, in their own languages, setting out our values, our goals, and our strategy. We cannot overcome a thousand years of insecurity and failure of their societies by talking, but we can blunt the jihadist propaganda by getting information out to those most in need of it. The U.S. Information Agency—disbanded with the fall of the Soviet Union—should be re-created for that mission. But that is only one step. It is essential that we defeat jihadism in a way that proves—like the freedom of Poland proved to Communists—that the success of jihadism is neither irreversible nor inevitable.

Toppling [Saddam Hussein's] regime in Iraq was irrelevant to defeating jihadist ideology. To disprove its inevitability and irreversibility, we must remove the jihadist regimes so that for at least two generations no hope of their revival seems possible. Of the jihadist regimes, Iran is by far the most dangerous. If its nuclear ambitions are realized—and they soon will be—the advent of nuclear terrorism will quickly follow. If [the September 11, 2001 terrorist attack] was the challenge of Mr. Bush's first term, Iran is the challenge of his second.

Iran Supports Terrorism

Since 1979, when Jimmy Carter watched while the Shah's regime was overthrown and the current kakistocracy [government by the worst] took power, Iran wasted no time in building a web of terrorist organizations to act upon its enmity toward America. Hezbollah, Iranian-created, equipped, and funded, made a battlefield of Beirut [Lebanon]. In 1983, at Iran's direction, a Hezbollah attack killed 241 Marines in the

Beirut barracks bombing. They kidnapped, tortured, and murdered Marine Lt. Col. William "Rich" Higgins, and CIA [Central Intelligence Agency] station chief William Buckley. Hezbollah fighters have been in Iraq, fighting beside the insurgents against Coalition troops. In Iraq, Iran has funded and operated the Moqtada al-Sadr "mahdi militia" and used it to attack and kill Coalition troops. Iran is now openly allied with [worldwide terrorist group] al Qaeda.

In May 2003, when a rocket attack on a civilian compound in Riyadh [Saudi Arabia] killed a number of Westerners, the Saudis were quick to blame outsiders. All eyes turned to Iran. Did the al Qaeda attack in Riyadh emanate from Iran? Defense Secretary Donald Rumsfeld said, "Well, I'll leave the analysis to others, but just from a factual standpoint, there is no question but that there have been, and there are today, senior al Qaeda leaders in Iran. And they are busy."

Reliable reports, including those related in Richard Miniter's [book] *Shadow War*, say that [al Qaeda leader] Osama bin Laden may be operating and traveling in Afghanistan and Iran under the protection of Iranian intelligence. According to Miniter's sources, this results from an agreement between bin Laden and Iranian grand ayatollah Ali Khameni after bin Laden sought sanctuary from the American attack on Afghanistan. Iran has admitted to harboring about 500 al Qaeda leaders, supposedly under arrest. Convenient jailbreaks (December 14, 2003) and transfer of some to Saudi custody (March 2003) probably arranged the release of most or all who were in custody. To call Iran a terrorist nation is a great understatement. It is the epicenter of Islamic jihadism, and its ambitions to global power will soon be vouchsafed by European appeasement.

Dangerous Agreements

Under the Nuclear Non-Proliferation Treaty (NPT) Iran is entitled to "peaceful" use of nuclear power. But a nation that sits on about 94 billion barrels of oil and some 25 trillion cubic meters of natural gas doesn't need nuclear power to generate electricity. It is building nuclear weapons and developing missiles to threaten any nation that would impose limits on its jihadist agenda. A nuclear Iran, with the means to deliver its weapons, would be able to increase its support for al Qaeda and their ilk with impunity. Any nation that would interfere with Iran's terrorist operations would risk nuclear war. And Mullah Strangelove[2] wouldn't hesitate to arm terrorists with nuclear weapons. For just those reasons, President Bush has said that Tehran will not be permitted to possess nuclear weapons. Iran has been lying about its nuclear weapons program to the International Atomic Energy Agency (IAEA), the U.N.'s purblind nuclear "watchdog," for about two decades.

Three EU [European Union] nations—Britain, France, and Germany—have been negotiating an endless stream of agreements with Iran which are supposed to give Iran better trade relations as the price for its ceasing to develop nuclear weapons. When Iran violates each agreement, the EU-3 step up and negotiate another. The EU-3 have apparently accepted the fact of a nuclear Iran, and Iran is playing them—and the U.N.—like well-hooked fish. [U.S.] Undersecretary of State John Bolton has been pressing the IAEA to report Iran's apparent violations of the NPT to the U.N. Security Council, with a view toward imposing diplomatic sanctions on Tehran. But every time America presses the IAEA, Iran talks to its European appeasers, and cuts us off at the diplomatic pass. Just last fall [2004] it happened again.

In November, when we pushed for U.N. debate on Iran's nukes, the Europeans negotiated another agreement with Iran. Under their November 15 agreement, Iran promises suspension of its nuclear program in return for continued negotiation on long-term economic benefits to Iran.

2. A reference to the 1960s movie *Dr. Strangelove*, a satire on nuclear war.

This agreement is exceedingly dangerous for many reasons. The least obvious is that the EU-3 "recognize that the suspension [of uranium enrichment, a key step in developing fissionable material] is a voluntary confidence-building measure and not a legal obligation." In diplo-speak, that means the EU nations have agreed that what Iran is doing—weapons-related or not—is legal for it to do. On that basis, the IAEA again decided everything in Iran is tickety-boo, and went back to sleep. While the IAEA sleeps, the Iranian nuclear and missile programs go on. Iran plans its first satellite launch in 2005.[3] If it succeeds, Iran's missiles will be proved capable of shooting objects into orbit, which means their soon-to-be-had nuclear arsenal will be able to reach essentially any nation.

We Must Be More Ruthless

Conventional wisdom says that our only options to deal with Iran are U.N. diplomacy or full-scale invasion. The first is useless, the second beyond our reach. We must choose to be less conventional and more ruthless in order to reach the necessary result in the short time we have. Iran may have nuclear weapons in less than two years. Some sources say that it already has one to three weapons, and is working hard to mate them to its missiles.

Tucked away in the November [2004] EU-3 agreement is the sentence, "Irrespective of the nuclear issue, the E-3/EU and Iran confirmed their determination to combat terrorism, including the activities of al Qaeda and groups such as the Mujahideen e-Khalq." It is impossible to conceive of any Western government agreeing to that sentence without the assistance of hallucinogens. The EU-3, floating along like [1960s LSD promoter] Timothy Leary, have affirmed that the central jihadist nation is combating terrorism. But the rest of that

3. Iran successfully launched an orbiting satellite in October 2005.

statement—referring to an otherwise obscure Iranian opposition group—shows how much the Mujahideen e-Khalq (MEK) frightens the mullahs.

The Status of MEK

MEK is a nominally-Communist Iranian opposition group that's on America's list of foreign terrorist organizations. And why is the MEK on our terrorist list? Because, in 1999, the Iranian government asked us to list them. According to the October 9, 1999 *Los Angeles Times*, "One senior Clinton administration official said inclusion of the [MEK] was intended as a goodwill gesture to Tehran . . ." Only the Clinton administration could slap the label "terrorist" on a group at the request of the principal terrorist regime in the whole bloody world. But any group that causes such great fear among the mullahs can't be all bad.

American forces bombed MEK positions in Iraq on one day in April 2003, trying to deprive Iran of an excuse to move its forces into Iraq. A month later, MEK voluntarily surrendered to American forces more than 2,000 tanks, artillery pieces, and armored vehicles, and some 3,800 MEK fighters are now in American custody at Camp Ashraf, north of Baghdad.

According to a July 21, 2004 letter to the "people of Ashraf," Gen. Geoffrey Miller—then deputy commanding general of multi-national forces in Iraq—informed the MEK members and their families at Camp Ashraf that they have been declared "protected persons" under the Geneva Conventions. By definition, that means they cannot be terrorists. Moreover, Miller's letter says that they have signed an agreement renouncing terrorism. MEK hasn't committed a terrorist act against American interests for about 25 years. . . . Secretary of State Condoleezza Rice should order an immediate review of MEK's status with a view toward taking them off the terrorist list. Once that's done, we can—secretly, and through proxies—rearm them and put them back in action against Tehran.

There are other options we can exercise against Iran. Air strikes on their nuclear weapons surface sites won't stop the program, but can slow Iran's progress for months or years. We should not hesitate to do it. Our B-2s can get in and out without the Iranians having a clue until it's too late. Some, including former Secretary of State Lawrence Eagleburger, decry military action as unlikely to stop the program. But they offer no better idea to slow it for sufficient time for opposition groups—such as MEK and Iranian would-be revolutionaries—to gather strength and oust the mullahs.

*"If the United States . . . bombs Iran's
civil nuclear facilities, . . . that will provoke a new, violent cycle of confrontation."*

The United States
Should Not Use Military
Strikes to End Iran's
Nuclear Weapons Program

Paul Rogers

*A military confrontation with Iran would lead to a cycle of vio-
lence, Paul Rogers maintains in the following viewpoint. He argues that Iran believes it has the right to develop nuclear weapons and would respond to a U.S. attack on its nuclear facilities
by becoming more involved in the war in Iraq and encouraging
terrorist attacks in Israel. According to Rogers, if the United
States uses force against Iran, the violence between the two nations would be impossible to reverse. Rogers is the global security
correspondent at OpenDemocracy.net.*

Paul Rogers, "Iran and the United States: A Clash of Perceptions," Opendemocracy
(www.opendemocracy.net), November 3, 2005. Reproduced by permission of Pluto Publishing Ltd.

As you read, consider the following questions:

1. How many diplomats has Iran recalled, according to Rogers?
2. In the author's view, how could Iran create an oil-market panic?
3. What was the problem with the U.S. policy in Iraq, according to Jake Lynch, as cited by Rogers?

The recent, rapid deterioration in relations between Iran and western European countries is only partly as a result of [Iranian president] Mahmoud Ahmadinejad's outspoken comments on 26 October [2005] about Israel. It also stems from a hardening of the Iranian line on the nuclear issue and, more significantly, the recall of as many as forty key diplomats. The diplomatic purge includes the ambassadors in London, Paris and Berlin, and those at the United Nations in New York and Geneva.

The significance of the decisions made so far is already clear: The people recalled are the very ones who have been involved in the nuclear negotiations, including some regarded as pragmatists more aligned with the president of an earlier era, Hashemi Rafsanjani (1989–97), than with the man who defeated him in the June election, Mahmoud Ahmadinejad.

These diplomatic changes come at a time of political uncertainty within the regime, not least with the failure of Ahmadinejad to get a number of ministerial appointees approved by the *majlis* (parliament). The fact that he has now chosen the notably inexperienced Sadeq Mahsuli for the key post of oil minister may have much to do with Mahsuli's earlier role as a Revolutionary Guard commander; it certainly suggests that the administration being formed is both inward-looking and callow, especially in international affairs.

Not an Ideal Situation

The current military situation isn't ideal for the United States:

- Historian John Lewis Gaddis notes that the shaky intelligence that buttressed the case for war in Iraq has "diminished, in advance, the credibility of whatever future intelligence claims Bush might make."

- Likely targets inside Iran are dispersed across the country—a country four times larger than Iraq—and many nuclear targets are simply unknown.

- After two wars, two nation-building operations, two counterinsurgencies and an ongoing global hunt for [the terrorist group] al-Qaeda's remnants, the U.S. military is showing signs of wear and tear.

Alan W. Dowd, American Legion, *November 2005.*

Neo-conservative Goals

At the same time, these current developments in Tehran must be seen in the context of the exceedingly sharp differences of outlook between Washington and Tehran. These differences are far more deep-seated than contingent political tensions and—as far as Iran is concerned—stretch beyond the Tehran regime to include large sectors of Iranian public opinion.

The [George W.] Bush administration persists in regarding Iran as the most significant member of the "axis of evil". The Saddam Hussein regime may have been terminated in Iraq, but Iran was always regarded as the more serious problem for Washington—and for its Israeli ally also. At a conference in Washington a few months after [the September 11, 2001 terrorist attacks], when early talk of attacking Iraq was circulating, one member of the Bush transition team spoke for many on the neo-conservative right when he said: "if we get Iraq right, we won't have to worry about Iran."

The logic was plain: to extinguish the Iraqi regime, install a client government and maintain troops in the country would surely have the effect of making Tehran very careful of its actions, thus aiding the United States's position in the region—to the extent that, whatever regime might govern in Iran, overthrowing it might not even be necessary.

A Clash of Perceptions

Although Iraq has not gone according to the US's plan, the Bush administration retains its strongly held view—one that derives from the traumatic 1979–80 period encompassing the downfall of the Shah, the violent convulsions of the Iranian revolution and, in particular, the hostage crisis—that Iran is the real problem. In particular, it is entirely unacceptable for Washington that any regime in Tehran should be allowed to get within reach of even a theoretical nuclear capability.

This emphatic judgment collides with an equally strong belief on the Iranian side, one that crosses most political boundaries, that the country has every right to develop nuclear power and nuclear weapons. The idea of Iran as one of the world's great states, with more than 4,000 years of civilisation, is embedded in Iranian society. This view is reinforced by more recent developments: Iran has seen regimes to its east (Afghanistan) and west (Iraq) destroyed by a superpower that describes it as "evil", permanent US bases being constructed in these neighbouring states, and its entire coastline effectively dominated by the US fifth fleet.

This fundamental clash of perceptions between Washington and Tehran shows no sign of diminishing. Indeed, the current Iranian rhetoric simply makes it easier for the United States (or Israel) to consider the use of force if diplomacy fails to fix the nuclear issue. The problem for these prospective assailants is that any such action might entail serious and unexpected escalation.

Iran would have several options in the event of a US or Israeli attack: direct Revolutionary Guard involvement across the border in Iraq, making the predicament of US forces almost impossible; encouraging [terrorist organization] Hizbollah to open a "Lebanon front" with Israel; even the temporary closure of the Strait of Hormuz to create an oil-market panic. The stakes are therefore very high, and it will take some extraordinary efforts by diplomats, mediators and others—including the Russians—to encourage the Washington and Tehran administrations to acquire a realistic sense of each other's point of view.

The High Cost of a Military Strike

Meanwhile, George Bush's conduct of his "war on terror" and his sundry domestic problems have encouraged Washington political analysts to suggest that neo-conservatism and the ideal of the New American Century have had their day—and that the logical result must be some serious rethinking of the Iraq imbroglio. The problem with this line of thinking is that the second simply does not follow the first. It is certainly possible that neo-conservatism may be in trouble (though it is far too early to write an obituary), but this in itself would not create space for rethinking on Iraq.

The problem for the United States is that the occupation of Iraq, the permanent military bases and the wished-for client regime in Baghdad are primarily about the wider control of the region's energy resources. It is possible that the US might have secured its influence in the region by other means than war, but the enforced termination of the Saddam Hussein regime has created a profound ratcheting effect. The United States cannot just change the tactics it has committed itself to, for they carry the necessary consequence of using even more force to control their own destructive effects. Jake

Lynch, co-author of *Peace Journalism*, expresses it well: Iraq was all about an entry strategy, but nowhere had an exit strategy as part of the policy.

This is where Iran is so significant. If the US/Iran crisis escalates to the point of military confrontation, the ratchet effect will become even more pronounced. If the United States (or Israel) bombs Iran's civil nuclear facilities in the next year or so, setting back a putative nuclear-weapons programme by several years, that will provoke a new, violent cycle of confrontation that, as with Iraq, cannot be reversed. Once force is used, it cannot be "unused".

When the United States decided to eradicate the Saddam regime in Iraq, the stakes were high on all sides. The price is now being paid. The potential price is even higher if war is waged on Iran, but that may not stop it happening. Indeed, the current increase in tension, including Mahmoud Ahmadinejad's comments, makes war more likely.

> *"The U.S. and Europe need to harmo-
> nize their approaches and develop a
> coordinated strategy for Iran."*

The United States Must Work with Europe to Control Iran

Alan L. Isenberg

*In the following viewpoint Alan L. Isenberg contends that if the
U.S. government wants to end Iran's quest to develop nuclear
weapons, it must work in harmony with European allies. He
contends that the United States and Europe must agree on the
consequences Iran will face if it reneges on its promises not to
build nuclear arms. Isenberg adds that the U.S. government
needs to become more involved with Iran and show Iranians
that the United States will be an ally of Iran should it become a
democracy. Isenberg is a writer for* Newsweek International *and
a former fellow at the Center for International Security and Cooperation at the Stanford Institute for International Studies.*

As you read, consider the following questions:

1. What does Isenberg consider problematic about Richard
   L. Armitage's view on Iran?
2. According to the author, what did European foreign
   ministers do in June 2003?

Alan L. Isenberg, "Want to Stop the Nukes? Make Nice," *Los Angeles Times*, November
28, 2004, p. M6. Reproduced by permission.

3. When were relations between Iran and the United States severed, in Isenberg's view?

We've been down this road before: A crisis threatens global security, and the international community is not coming together to deal with it. Hawks in the U.S. administration see the Europeans as too timid to use force and reliant on diplomacy to a fault, while many Europeans see the United States as trigger-happy and too impatient with negotiated settlements. This lack of cohesion damaged the legitimacy of the American-led war in Iraq and left U.S.-European relations in tatters. A similar disunity jeopardizes current attempts to manage Iran's nuclear aspirations, even though both sides agree that the threat posed by a nuclear Iran is grave and real.

Good Cop/Bad Cop

Departing Deputy Secretary of State Richard L. Armitage positively spun the divergent U.S. and European approaches to Iran: "The [diplomatic] incentives of the Europeans," he said, "only work against the backdrop of the United States being strong and firm on this issue. In the vernacular, it's kind of a good cop/bad cop arrangement. If it works, we'll all have been successful." The problem with Armitage's hopeful outlook is that the good cop/bad cop strategy works only if pursued consciously and in coordination, and the U.S. and European approaches do not reflect that yet. In fact, they seem headed in opposite directions.

The good cops—Britain, France and Germany—recently persuaded Iran to suspend all uranium enrichment-related activities until they reach a final accord. If the mullahs cooperate, they will receive numerous economic carrots, including possible membership in the World Trade Organization (the U.S. would have to agree) and improved trade relations.

In October 2003, when the International Atomic Energy Agency [IAEA] was prepared to take its negative report on

Defeating Iran's Efforts

The U.S. and its friends must do much more than they are currently doing to frustrate Iran's efforts to divide the U.S., Israel, and Europe from one another, as well as from other friends in the Middle East and Asia, and to defeat Tehran's efforts to use its nuclear capabilities to deter others from taking firm action against Iranian misbehavior.

Henry Sokolski, Policy Review, *June/July 2005.*

Iran's nuclear program to the U.N. [United Nations] Security Council, the mullahs cut a similar deal with the Europeans, promising to suspend all enrichment-related activities. But Iran soon grew impatient with the agreement and resumed efforts to produce the gas that feeds uranium enrichment. It similarly rushed to make as much of that gas as possible before the latest accord's deadline, undercutting confidence in the deal on both sides of the Atlantic. In another bad-faith move, Iran announced [in November 2004] that it wanted to keep operating uranium-enrichment equipment for research purposes, backing off its pledge to freeze all such activities.

Enter the bad cop—the United States. It has pushed to refer the question of Iran's nuclear aspirations to the Security Council. When Secretary of State Colin L. Powell steps down, the hawkish voices in his department will probably intensify and gain influence, especially if the mullahs break the newest deal.

Armitage might be right that the discordant U.S.-European approaches will push the mullahs to hold to the deal. But the U.S. will be uncomfortable with an agreement that does not insist on any means of enforcement or verification, as is the case with the latest accord.

The United States and Europe Must Cooperate

Iran knows that the war in Iraq colors U.S. conduct toward it. The worse Iraq gets, the less Iran worries—and the mullahs don't seem too worried at the moment. But if they break the accord with the Europeans and the Europeans respond timidly and U.S. resources are freed up as a result of an improving situation in Iraq, the U.S. could take on Iran alone—to everyone's detriment. To avoid this risk, the U.S. and Europe need to harmonize their approaches and develop a coordinated strategy for Iran. The best way to accomplish this is to agree in advance on the consequences Iran will face if it violates its commitments. For example, if the mullahs renege on the latest deal, frustrate the monitoring and verification efforts of IAEA inspectors or fail to ratify an addition to the Nuclear Non-Proliferation Treaty that allows for more invasive inspections, the U.S. and Europe should go to the Security Council, impose economic sanctions or, in the worst case, take military action.

Fortunately, diplomatic disunity over Iran does not run as deep as it did over Iraq, where even the nature of the threat was a bone of contention. Both the U.S. and Europe are worried about a nuclear Iran, and they feel strongly about enforcing the rules of nonproliferation. In June 2003, European foreign ministers required only 45 minutes to approve a document that endorsed U.N.-sanctioned use of force as a last resort against proliferators, as well as "political and diplomatic preventative measures."

If the Europeans agree to leave all responses on the table and to act decisively at the first sign of Iranian mischief, the United States would be foolish not to form a partnership with them. (It's also important that the U.S. set a better example as a member of the nonproliferation community by abandoning plans to build new mini-nuclear weapons and ratifying the Comprehensive Test Ban Treaty.)

Working with Iran

The role the U.S. forges for itself in dealing with Iran will have significance beyond reinvesting in international order or responding to the mullahs' nuclear ambitions. Iran's despotic regime will collapse some day, and there will be a "morning after" similar to that in Iraq, where reconstruction efforts have floundered because U.S. planners underestimated the challenge of nation-building and the need for international support to make it work. When Iran makes its move toward a better government, the U.S. should be in a position to lead a coherent, collective international effort to help it get off the ground.

Yet since the severing of U.S.-Iranian ties in 1980, the U.S. has been slack in developing a viable Iran policy. Iran's nuclear ambition should be motive enough to reverse this inattention. U.S. policy toward Iran must cease to be reactive, as it is now.

In addition to working with the Europeans to curb the mullahs' nuclear efforts, the U.S. should begin crafting a strategy to work toward—and then with—a democratic Iran. Supporting a government that complies with its international obligations is certainly preferable to containing one that thwarts them. By getting involved now, the U.S. can do much to show Iranians that it will be a friend to a free Iran. A democratic Iran may still want a nuclear bomb as a matter of national pride. But a less threatening, pro-diplomacy U.S. would be in a stronger position to argue the benefits of membership in the nonproliferation community rather than life as a rogue power.

Participating in a multilateral approach to Iran's nuclear program is a great place to start. In doing so, the U.S. will signal to Iranians that its aggressive position does not reflect a desire to remake Iran in its own image but rather a desire to achieve, alongside Europe, a substantial victory for nonproliferation and international security.

> "Since including Iran in the original 'axis of evil' in 2002, Mr. Bush has softened his rhetoric on Iran to a near-whisper."

The United States Should Not Follow Europe's Lead on Iran

The Wall Street Journal

In the following viewpoint the Wall Street Journal *contends that European efforts at diplomacy have failed to derail Iran's plans to develop nuclear weapons. The editors argue that the United States must stop taking a back seat to Europe regarding Iranian affairs. The newspaper claims that Iran has become increasingly dangerous, supporting terrorism in Iraq and continuing to engage in a uranium enrichment process in order to build nuclear arms. According to the* Journal, *the United States must consider other options such as military intervention rather than to support the weak and ineffective diplomatic efforts of Europe. The* Wall Street Journal *is a daily newspaper that focuses on business and politics.*

As you read, consider the following questions:

1. According to the author, how many candidates were barred from participating in Iran's 2005 election?
2. What did an internal Iranian government document reveal, as quoted by the *Wall Street Journal*?
3. Why does the author oppose economic sanctions?

For two years now, the Bush Administration has willingly taken a back seat to European diplomacy to induce Iran to abandon its nuclear-weapons program. In the [summer of 2005], the world has been able to see what this non-cowboy strategy has achieved:

- Iran's new president [Mahmoud Ahmadinejad] has called for "a wave of Islamic revolution." Only a few years ago, this new world statesman was running gangs of street thugs who harassed anti-government demonstrators. His political rise was engineered by Supreme Leader Ayatollah Khameini, who barred 1,000 reformist candidates from the recent parliamentary elections.

- [In August 2005,] Iranian police opened fire on a peaceful demonstration of Iranian Kurds in the city of Mahabad, reportedly killing four of the protestors. Meanwhile, dissident journalist Akbar Ganji is on . . . a prison hunger strike, and prosecutors are now threatening his family.

- On the nuclear issue, Tehran has resumed an early-stage uranium enrichment process at its nuclear site in Isfahan. And it has denounced as "unacceptable" a European offer to provide security and economic favors in exchange for Iran dropping parts of its nuclear program that have bomb-making uses.

MEMRI [Middle East Media Research Institute], which translates Middle East broadcasts from their native languages, recently captured Iran's chief nuclear negotiator, Hosein Musavian, on Iranian TV: "Thanks to the negotiations with Europe, we gained another year, in which we completed" Isfahan. Iran suspended enrichment "in Isfahan in October 2004, although we were required to do so in October 2003. . . . Today we are in a position of power. We have a stockpile of products, and during this period we have managed to convert 36 tons of yellowcake into gas and store it."

Exploiting America and Europe

Then there is Iranian assistance for terrorists in Iraq. Defense Secretary Donald Rumsfeld has publicly accused Iran of "allowing" weapons to move across its Western border, and U.S. troops have captured explosives shaped for destructive terror use with Iranian pedigrees. *Time* magazine, no friend of the U.S. effort in Iraq, recently published a report, "Inside Iran's Secret War for Iraq." This is all especially notable because advocates of courting the mullahs often warn that a harder line against Tehran could invite Iranian meddling in Iraq. But that meddling is a reality under current Iran policy, and it is killing American soldiers.

The Iranians themselves are now admitting that all of this is no happenstance but is a calculated effort to exploit what the mullahs perceive to be American weakness and Europe's lack of will. An internal Iranian government document recently obtained by an opposition group says that "The talks process ended the suffocating economic pressures that our country was being subjected to in the months prior to the October 2003 agreement. . . . With the Americans deeply stuck in a quagmire in Iraq, the Europeans know that they will have to ultimately accommodate our just demands."

And why shouldn't the mullahs believe this, given Europe's reaction to President Bush's routine recent comments that "all options are on the table" regarding Iran's nuclear ambitions? German Chancellor Gerhard Schröder, facing an uphill elec-

Emboldening Iran

The so-called EU-3—Britain, France and Germany—have tried to appease the mullahs into giving up the nuclear weapons program that the Iranian regime is making less and less effort to conceal. Emboldened by the absence of real penalties (or, for that matter, any adverse consequences), Iranian spokesmen have taken to talking openly—and gleefully—about how European diplomacy has "bought time" to bring their nuclear program to fruition. Worse yet, they now have advertised their willingness to share Iran's nuclear technology with other Islamic nations.

Frank J. Gaffney Jr., FrontPagemagazine.com,
November 2, 2005. www.frontpagemagazine.com.

tion campaign, seized on the remark as an opportunity to repudiate even the possibility of using force. "We have seen it doesn't work," he declared, in a reference to Iraq. ([Deposed Iraqi leader] Saddam Hussein might argue from his holding cell that it does.)

Changing Strategies

No one can plausibly claim that this Iranian hardline has been inspired by U.S. saber-rattling. Since including Iran in the original "axis of evil" in 2002, Mr. Bush has softened his rhetoric on Iran to a near-whisper. The Administration agreed to European mediation efforts in October 2003, and agreed again in 2004 after Iran cheated on its initial commitments by secretly enriching uranium. Then the U.S. agreed again to another try earlier [in 2005], this time offering World Trade Organization membership. Tehran's response has been evident the last few weeks.

Perhaps it's time to try a different strategy. We aren't referring here to economic sanctions via the U.N. [United Nations]

Security Council. China and Russia aren't likely to agree to sanctions, and even if they did (after many months of haggling) Iran may think it can ride them out in a world of $60 oil. Leaving aside—but not ruling out—the option of military intervention, the Iranian regime is vulnerable to diplomatic pressure from without and even more so to democratic pressure from below. Yet the Bush Administration has given comparatively little support to Iranian pro-democracy groups, and it has made no effort to organize bans on Iranian participation in prestigious international forums or at sporting and cultural events. Patrick Clawson of the Washington Institute for Near East Policy suggests, for starters, barring the Iranian national soccer team from the World Cup.

Perhaps even this is too militant for the likes of Chancellor Schröder. But it would be the beginning of a serious Iran policy.

> *"Over the long run, Iran's democratic movement would benefit from greater contact with Western societies."*

The United States Should Encourage Political Reform in Iran

Michael McFaul and Abbas Milani

Democracy can succeed in Iran, particularly if the U.S. government supports Iran's democratic movement, Michael McFaul and Abbas Milani argue in the following viewpoint. The authors maintain, however, that Iranian reformists must first acknowledge that democracy is incompatible with religious rule and join the ranks of Iran's democratic reformers. The authors conclude that the United States should promote democracy by refusing to negotiate with Iran's conservative religious leaders and by providing moral support to Iranians working toward democracy. McFaul is the Helen and Peter Bing Senior Fellow at the Hoover Institution and an associate professor of political science at Stanford University. Milani is the codirector of the Iran Democracy Project at the Hoover Institution and a visiting professor of political science at Stanford University.

Michael McFaul and Abbas Milani, "Solidarity with Iran," *Hoover Digest*, no. 2, 2004, pp. 60–69. Copyright © 2004 by the board of trustees of the Leland Stanford Junior University. Reproduced by permission.

As you read, consider the following questions:

1. According to the authors, what percentage of eligible Iranian voters participated in the February 2004 elections?

2. What is the "China model," as defined by McFaul and Milani?

3. In the authors' view, what reassurance does Iran's democratic movement need from other democracies?

If President Bush is serious about promoting democracy in the greater Middle East, then a strategy to assist democratization in Iran should be a top priority. No country in the region, after all, is riper for a democratic breakthrough. At the same time, especially after the farcical parliamentary election in February [2004], Iranian democrats have entered a dark and difficult phase in the development of their struggle. Now more than ever they need clarity about American intentions and real demonstrations of commitment to the cause of Iranian democracy from their American counterparts.

A Farcical Election

Iran's parliamentary election, held on February 20, turned out to be a farce. It was, in effect, an electoral coup. Conservative clerics used their self-declared right to vet candidates to the parliament to eliminate more than 2,000 reformist candidates from running in the election. In at least 190 districts—easily more than half of all the seats in the parliament—they "approved" only conservative candidates, thus ensuring for themselves a clear majority in the parliament. . . .

The election in February was a major step backward. The reformers suffered a severe setback. Ayatollah [Ali] Khamenei—[Ayatollah Ruholla] Khomenei's successor as the real leader of Iran—handpicked members of the new parliament through the conservative-dominated Guardian Council, which has the authority to vet candidates. Furthermore, his handpicked members of the Guardian Council and parliament are likely to soon welcome his handpicked president; and then even the pretense of a republic will wither as the reality of the one-man rule becomes more apparent.

In discussing the election (dubbed the "Friday coup" for the day on which it was held), analysts have focused rightly on how the reformists were pushed aside in the electoral putsch. But the reality was more complicated. The most disenfranchised were of course the Iranian people, who were denied the chance to participate in fair and free elections. They showed their disgruntlement by their refusal to participate in the badly compromised process. Only 50 percent of eligible voters went to the polls, showing a drop of about 15 percent since the last national elections. Furthermore, pernicious but pervasive rumors about punishments meted out to those who did not vote—it was rumored, for instance, that a failure to vote could prevent one from getting admitted to a university—forced many of these outsiders to go to the voting polls. Even then, no more than 30 percent of Tehran's eligible voters went to the polls.

The Story Behind the Coup

Of the insiders, two other hitherto powerful factions were also victims, along with the reformists, in this electoral coup. Hashemi Rafsanjani, once reputed to be Iran's real "strongman," seems now to be altogether marginalized. Nearly all his cohorts and allies have been eliminated from the parliament, while relatives of Rafsanjani, including his brother who used to serve as the undersecretary for the oil ministry, have recently "retired."

The other group conspicuously absent from the newly elected parliament are members of the group called Mo'talefe, hitherto one of the pillars of Khamenei's power and the bastion of conservative fundamentalism. Mo'talefe—originally a covert terrorist group established in the early 1960s to fight

Financial Support Can Help Spur Democracy

United States sanctions . . . prevent any American person or group from financially supporting, say, a microfinance bank, a program to train future political leaders or even an education initiative for rural women in Iran. That is a mistake. Elsewhere in the Middle East, the United States has programs that provide exactly these kinds of grants, in the name of democratization.

The United States should ease such sanctions in order to match its rhetorical commitment to Iranian democracy with meaningful action.

Afshin Molavi, New York Times, *November 3, 2005.*

the Shah, which has turned into an ostensibly overt "political" party only in recent months—had also been the conduit between the traditional bazaar and the top brass of the clergy. In other words, the February election was not only a big setback for the reformers and the people of Iran but also a major blow to conservative factions within the regime. Power has now been consolidated around one man—Ayatollah Khamenei.

What then is the reason for this coup, and what does it mean for the future of democracy in Iran and the region? The attempt to consolidate power in the hands of one man is less a sign of systemic power than a sign of weakness. The regime knows that it is entering a perilous period and that its very survival is on the line. Concentrated leadership, it thinks, will help it navigate the increasingly inhospitable waters. Rid of the rigid cultural politics of the conservatives, on the one hand, and of the political embarrassments brought about by widespread rumors of financial corruption by Rafsanjani and members of his family, on the other, Khamenei hopes to have a better chance of solving the crisis. If the International Atomic Energy Agency produces another damning report of lies and deceptions in the regime's nuclear program, it will be more difficult for the regime's European allies to continue their engagement with this autocratic regime. Recent comments by the European Union's spokesperson criticizing the recent elections are early hints of a possible rift with Europe. The regime's internal isolation will be complemented by its international isolation when Europe decides to align itself with Iran's democratic movement rather than its despotic rulers.

How the Reformists Can Respond

The sine qua non of this movement has been the principle that democracy and the rule of an all-powerful "spiritual leader" (the position held by Khamenei) are simply incompatible. Hitherto many of the reformists harbored illusions about this fact. In the now memorable phrase of Said Hajjariyan, one of the leaders of the reform movement, their formula for change was simple: "pressure from below, haggle at the top." In other words, they hoped to use the pressure for democratic change brought to bear by students, journalists, women, and members of the middle and working classes to get a bigger piece of the political pie for their group of insiders and lessen the chance of a popular eruption. What they have now realized is that the mullahs at the top do not play by any rules, save those that serve their interests. Dismayed and disappointed by how little their "haggling" accomplished, they now have an opportunity of joining the democratic forces.

With these reformists—who are an important segment of Iranian society—now finally ready to cut the cord from the Islamic regime, they can join the ranks of the democratic movement, making it both more representative and more powerful. For several years, the reformers had one foot in the regime and one foot in society. Now they have been pushed out of the regime and must stand firmly with democratic forces in society.

In this new polarized context, the regime's only hope, and arguably its ultimate plan, is to make peace with the United States, and rely on that peace to improve the country's dire economic conditions. The regime hopes to follow the "China model," mixing economic recovery with an authoritarian political system. President Bush's criticisms of the February elections are a hopeful sign that the administration will not fall prey to the temptation of making a deal . . . with the masterminds of the coup.

For most Americans, Iran is viewed as a totalitarian regime, not unlike other dictatorships in the region and not that different from the other remaining member of the axis of evil, North Korea. In reality, Iranian society is one of the most pluralist—and its Islamic rule the most tenuous—in the region, and the prospects for a democratic breakthrough are greater there than anywhere else in the autocratic Muslim world. . . .

Promoting Democracy

The current political crisis underscores yet again the unique opportunity in Iran for democratic regime change. And if democracy succeeds in Iran, the positive reverberations around the region, including in Iraq and Afghanistan, will be enormous.

The first and most important step in executing a new strategy for promoting democracy in Iran is to clarify the United States' position vis-à-vis the current Iranian regime. The recent elections—and the loss of any semblance of a democracy within the power structure—make this task easier now than in the past.

President Bush issued a bold statement of solidarity with the Iranian people a few days after the electoral coup. The administration must make clear that the United States has no intention of pursuing closer ties with Khamenei and his minions as a reward for dismantling their nuclear weapons program or for their promise of "cooperation" in keeping Iraqi Shiites calm.

The Bush administration cannot be tempted into entering into negotiations with Khamenei or his surrogates. Bush and his administration must initiate a more sophisticated and comprehensive strategy for engaging Iranian society. Most immediately, democratic forces in Iran need moral support from their friends in the West. They want to be reassured that the international community of democracies, including the United States, is still on their side. As a simple gesture of solidarity, President Bush should deliver a major speech devoted to Iranian democracy.

The West Can Help Improve Iran

Over the long run, Iran's democratic movement would benefit from greater contact with Western societies, more exposure to Western ideas, and more integration with Western economies. The same strategy and organizations that helped to engage Polish society (well, save the Catholic Church) must be deployed in Iran.

The future of Iran, and its long-cherished hope of democracy, must and will be determined inside Iran. But the United States can play a crucial role by siding with the democratic aspirations of the Iranian people.

"*The point on which most [Iranians] agree is that fundamental reform must come about peacefully and without U.S. interference.*"

The United States Must Not Become Involved in Iranian Political Reform

Geneive Abdo

In the following viewpoint Geneive Abdo contends that the United States should not become involved with democratization efforts in Iran. She maintains that the substantial powers of Iran's supreme clerical leader make Iran a nation hostile to Western secular democracy. It is clear, Abdo concludes, that U.S. efforts to aid democratic reforms in Iran will fail. Abdo is an author and journalist who specializes in articles and books on contemporary Islam, including Answering Only to God: Faith and Freedom in Twenty-First Century Iran.

As you read, consider the following questions:

1. In the author's view, how is the political situation in modern Iran markedly different than it was in 1979?

Geneive Abdo, "Stay Out of Iran," *Washington Post National Weekly Edition*, June 30–July 13, 2003, p. 26. Reproduced by permission.

2. As explained by Abdo, what powers does the supreme clerical leader possess?

3. Why is the author critical of America's involvement in the overthrow of Iran's government in 1953?

The [2003] student protests in the Iranian capital, Tehran, have quickened the collective pulse in Washington among those eagerly awaiting "regime change" in the Islamic republic.

President Bush has welcomed what he called popular demands for a "free Iran." Administration officials and their neoconservative allies have proclaimed that the Iranian people are at last acting on their calls to overthrow the ruling mullahs. Switch on CNN or Fox News and listen to Iranian exiles gleefully declare that the collapse of clerical power could be only months away.

Revolution Is Unlikely

But is Iran, once the center of radical Islam, really ripe for another revolution? Has it reached what Secretary of Defense Donald Rumsfeld likes to call a "tipping point," ready to fall with the slightest push? Neither history nor contemporary facts on the ground support such conclusions.

In marked contrast to the run-up to the 1979 Islamic Revolution,[1] the fruit of what has been called a "theology of discontent" created over many decades by disparate factions, politics in Iran today remains very much the preserve of a narrow circle of "insiders." These revolutionaries, comprising so-called reformers and hard-liners alike, have no intention of easing their shared monopoly on power.

The result is the complete lack of any credible opposition political movement or cohesive ideological challenge to the current Islamic political system. Restive students, often identi-

1. In 1979 Muhammad Reza Shah Pahlavi, the U.S.–backed ruler of Iran, fled the nation in response to popular unrest over his policies. The shah was replaced by the Ayatollah Ruholla Khomeini, who moved the nation toward Islamic conservatism.

A Military Attack Would Hinder Democracy

In the following interview excerpt, Stephen Shalom, a professor of political science at William Paterson University in New Jersey, comments on the impact of a military attack on Iran.

Would an attack help or hinder Iran's pro-democracy movement? Would an attack be welcomed in Iran? What is the state of that movement?

Stephen Shalom: People in all countries tend to rally around the flag when under attack, especially when the attack is not aimed against dictatorship, but against weapons which the Iranian population knows are possessed by others. The reform movement in Iran is currently quite weak, and an atmosphere of jingoism in the face of foreign encirclement and attack will not help it.

Stephen Shalom, interviewed by Jason Schulman,
Democratic Left, *Spring 2005.*

fied by the Bush administration as those who might lead an internal rebellion, remain few and have repeatedly failed to turn their street demonstrations into a broad-based opposition movement. Simply put, there is no viable alternative on the horizon.

Vast Clerical Power

At the same time, Iran's constitution concentrates enormous power in the hands of the supreme clerical leader, appointed by conservative clerics. This includes command of the armed forces, control over the secret police and the courts, and the authority to confirm or reject the election of the president.

Backed by such institutional authority, and able to call on legions of Islamic vigilantes and other supporters sworn to uphold absolute clerical rule, supreme leader Ayatollah Ali Khamenei has little to fear from the Iranian "street." Militant hard-liners recently burst into a university dormitory and beat students as they slept.

The beatings were a repeat of 1999, when foot soldiers of Khamenei rampaged through a student hostel, igniting five days of protests in which thousands of students nationwide staged the largest demonstrations since the 1979 revolution. The ease with which those 1999 protests were suppressed and the brutality of the subsequent repression have helped ensure any threat will remain in the background for years to come.

America Should Not Become Involved

The "pact" the Bush administration and its allies in Congress claim to have established with the disenchanted Iranian nation against its own leaders is a pure fabrication, one that plays into the hands of clerical hard-liners by allowing them to paint their opponents as U.S. stooges.

Iranians do want change, but the point on which most agree is that fundamental reform must come about peacefully and without U.S. interference. Besides, it is certain that whatever might emerge in a post-clerical Iran would not resemble a Western-style, secular democracy but would instead take into account Iranians' deeply felt commitment to Islam.

[In the summer of 2002], the White House publicly abandoned any hopes for Iran's official reform movement, led by President Mohammad Khatami, and called on the Iranian people to push for political and social change on their own. With nothing to show for the intervening months, the administration is now groping toward a new strategy to be encompassed in what is known as a "national security directive."

The document, now circulating in competing drafts, is classified, but there are worrisome signs it will draw heavily on the experience of the unfinished Iraq campaign and will likewise rely on a coalition of Washington hawks and exiles to see it through.

Already, the familiar refrain can be heard from administration figures: intimations of high-level Iranian complicity with al Qaeda [terrorists]; the development of weapons of mass destruction outside international safeguards; and reassuring strains from the expatriate elite that gruntled Iranians would welcome U.S.-inspired "regime change" with open arms.

Remembering Previous Lessons

U.S. officials now speak openly of deploying the armed Iranian opposition, allied with [former Iraqi leader] Saddam Hussein until his fall and listed by the State Department as a terrorist group, to pressure the Iranians. The son of the disgraced shah, who has no backing at home but enjoys the support of many in the diaspora and among Washington hawks, is already positioning himself for power.

If the chaos of postwar Iraq is not lesson enough, the administration would do well to ponder past experience with U.S.-led "regime change" in Iran; it is a sorry one, and there is nothing to suggest that things would be different this time. The CIA-inspired coup that ousted the elected government and restored the late shah to power in 1953 planted the seeds of the Islamic Revolution 25 years later, inflicting one of the greatest setbacks in U.S. diplomatic history.

It is likely a similar backlash could occur if the United States intervened once again in Iran.

Periodical Bibliography

The following articles have been selected to supplement the diverse views presented in this chapter.

Bruce Anderson	"Let Them Build Nukes," *Spectator*, August 13, 2005.
Ted Galen Carpenter	"Dealing with a Nuclear Iran," *Chronicles*, March 2005.
Alan W. Dowd	"Handle with Care: Iran, Nukes, and War," *American Legion*, November 2005.
Shirin Ebadi and Hadi Ghaemi	"The Human Rights Case Against Attacking Iran," *New York Times*, February 8, 2005.
Leon Hadar	"Target: Tehran?" *American Conservative*, November 22, 2004.
Robert E. Hunter	"Talk It Out on Iran Before It's Too Late," *Los Angeles Times*, August 27, 2004.
Issues and Controversies on File	"U.S.-Iran Relations Update," September 12, 2003.
Jeff Jacoby	"Iranian People Need Our Support," *Conservative Chronicle*, July 2, 2003.
Bob Long	"Will Iran Be the Next Quagmire?" *New Unionist News*, April 2005.
Jehangir Pocha	"Ally of Evil," *In These Times*, February 17, 2003.
Kenneth M. Pollack	"U.S. Is Needed to Defuse Iran," *Los Angeles Times*, November 17, 2004.
Saman Sepehri	"Will the U.S. Attack?" *International Socialist Review*, July/August 2005.

OPPOSING
VIEWPOINTS®
SERIES

CHAPTER 4

What Is the Future of Iran?

Chapter Preface

Discussions about the future of Iran often focus on whether the nation can become a democracy and whether it can improve its relationships with Europe and the United States. Another area in which Iran may experience significant changes, however, is its economy. Many Iranian leaders believe that the best path to a successful future is to model the nation after China; however, implementing the "China model," which emphasizes economic liberalization over political reforms, would require overcoming many challenges.

Those in Iran who wish to pattern the country after China face both political and social obstacles. Strategic consultant Bijian Khajehpour, writing for the Middle East Research and Information Project, argues that supporters of the Chinese model face opposition from ultrareformists and hard-line conservatives—the first group because they think political reforms should be attended to first, the latter group because they believe economic reforms such as opening up trade with other nations could weaken their political power by hurting the business monopolies that support the regime. Khajehpour contends that "while the centrist consensus may try to further marginalize the opposing currents, for the time being the balance of power is such that the ultrareformist and hard-line conservative forces will have the ability to undermine the political process."

In addition to threatening Iran's political leaders, the China model also poses a risk to the social fabric. As *San Francisco Chronicle* correspondent Borzou Daragahi observes, investing in foreign businesses will bring foreigners and their non-Muslim values to Iran. Consequently, Daragahi believes, Iran's social climate could change, which may alienate the nation's traditionalists. Daragahi notes, "Those forces might stymie the pragmatic conservatives' goal of a Chinese model, leaving them unable to solve Iran's myriad domestic problems."

Another problem with the China model is that Iran may not have the economic framework needed to match China's success. Afshin Molavi, writing for *Foreign Affairs*, asserts that the nation suffers from too many preexisting economic problems—such as corruption, U.S. economic sanctions, and an uncompetitive manufacturing sector—for such a model to succeed. According to Molavi, Iran will likely succeed only if it sets its goals lower and focuses on "creating limited economic openings that produce minor job growth and forestall unrest."

The future of Iran has significant consequences for the Middle East and the rest of the world. In the following chapter the authors debate the direction that Iran might take in the twenty-first century.

> "Ongoing political impasse, economic distress, and social turmoil . . . threaten the survival of the [Iranian] Islamic state."

Iranian Political Reform Is Likely

Jahangir Amuzegar

Iran's Islamic leadership is in decline, Jahangir Amuzegar claims in the following viewpoint. He argues that Iranians are becoming increasingly dissatisfied with the nation's economic struggles and the theocrats' intrusions into their daily life. Amuzegar asserts that increased civil disobedience and economic reforms may signal the end of the Islamic regime and help bring democracy to the nation. Amuzegar is an international economic consultant who served in Iran's government before the 1979 Islamic revolution.

As you read, consider the following questions:

1. In what way did the Ayatollah Taheri condemn Iran's Islamic regime, according to Amuzegar?

2. According to the author, what effects have demonstrations and strikes had in Iran?

Jahangir Amuzegar, "Iran's Crumbling Revolution," *Foreign Affairs*, January–February 2003, p. 44. Copyright © 2003 by the Council on Foreign Relations, Inc. All rights reserved. Reprinted by permission of the publisher, www.foreignaffairs.org.

3. According to Amuzegar, what must Iran do if it wants to become a full member of the World Trade Organization?

The United States should seize this moment to plan for Iran's political endgame because the regime's particular brand of politics and religion is in a state of ferment. At the same time, the government has been further weakened because it has failed to deliver on its promises of economic development.

Cracks in the Regime

Ayatollah Khomeini[1] built a governing ideology on concepts of independence, freedom, and the *velayat-e faqih*.[2] This fusion of statecraft with piety through the absolute power of a supreme leader (the rahbar) is now beginning to crumble. The first crack appeared in 1997 when the philosophy's principal architect, Grand Ayatollah Hossein Ali Montazeri, rejected the unquestioned power of the rahbar on the grounds that Islam forbids the supremacy of fallible humans. Emboldened by this attack on Khomeini's orthodoxy, a number of mid-ranking clerics and seminarians have subsequently denounced theocratic intrusion into daily life, refusing to accept the inviolability of the rahbar's religious edicts and even allowing fresh interpretations of the Koran itself. The new generation of clerics, taking their cue from older theologians such as Montazeri, now openly questions the legitimacy of absolutist religious power and even speaks of the need for an Islamic reformation. Some young seminarians in the holy city of Qom are now even questioning whether the unity of mosque and state is in their interest, since the unpopularity of the Islamic regime has reduced the number of clerics in the Majles [parlia-

1. The Ayatollah Ruholla Khomeini was the cleric who ruled Iran from the beginning of the 1979 Islamic revolution until his death in 1989.
2. This phrase means "rule of the Islamic jurist."

ment] and local councils and has also shrunk sources of private funding.

The latest condemnation of the regime came from Ayatollah [Jalaluddin] Taheri, who in July 2002, while resigning from his post as the leader of Friday prayers in Isfahan, lambasted the religious hard-liners for incompetence and corruption. The cleric, formerly a devoted Khomeini follower and an early revolutionary during the shah's time, bemoaned the host of social, political, and economic woes afflicting the country—from rising unemployment to growing drug addiction to increasing disregard for the law. No previous internal criticism of the theocratic regime had ever been this scathing. The response by the leadership was mostly dismissive. However, Supreme Leader [Ali] Khamenei, while complaining that this type of dissent would only embolden the regime's enemies, did acknowledge that he himself had pointed to some of the same shortcomings.

Trust in the power of Islamist ideology has declined even more profoundly as Khomeini's mixture of religion and politics has failed to deliver its promised rewards of prosperity and social justice. Despite a 100 percent rise in average annual oil income since the revolution, most indicators of economic welfare have steadily deteriorated. The so-called misery index (a combination of inflation and unemployment) has reached new highs. Average inflation in the years after the revolution has been at least twice as high as during the 1970s, unemployment has been three times higher, and economic growth is two-thirds lower. As a result, Iran's per capita income has declined by at least 30 percent since 1979. By official admission, more than 15 percent of the population now lives below the absolute poverty line, and private estimates run as high as 40 percent. A combination of slow growth, double-digit unemployment, high inflation, declining labor productivity, and increasing dependence on oil revenue has thus defied almost all government efforts to put the economy back on track. Although the alarming rate of population growth in the first decade after the revolution has been brought under control, both per capita income and domestic income distribution lag behind official targets. In short, the ailing economy has helped bring the regime's legitimacy further into question. A recent study leaked from Iran's Interior Ministry revealed that nearly 90 percent of the public is dissatisfied with the present government. Of this total, 28 percent wants "fundamental" changes in the regime's structure, and 66 percent desires "gradual reforms." Less than 11 percent—most probably those on the government dole—is satisfied with the status quo. Other private polls show an even greater degree of unhappiness with the government.

The combination of these two phenomena—the bankruptcy of Iran's ideology and the failure of its economy—now confronts the Islamic Republic with the worst challenge to its legitimacy yet. The public and the press now openly question the role of Islam—and especially the concept of the *velayat-e faqih*—in a society where people want greater freedom and the rule of law.

A Move Toward Democracy

Iran's conservative clerics are now helplessly witnessing a slow but steady drive toward democratization. Despite the political crackdown, legislative deadlock, and rumors of a coup, two provocative and parallel developments are challenging the mullahs' hegemony and paving the way for the regime's eventual collapse.

The first development relates to the expansion of civil society and the use of civil disobedience to loosen the theocracy's grip on national institutions. Nongovernmental organizations are being formed by the thousands, with and without official permission, to deal with ongoing problems ranging from family planning to drug addiction to pollution. Workers have formed informal (and extralegal) trade unions, and students

Internal Religious Conflicts

The ruling bloc in Iran has not been able to resolve its internal conflicts over economic, social, political, and moral issues by the physical or ideological elimination of one faction by another. Unable to replace the late Ayatollah [Khomeini] with an equally charismatic and powerful figure capable of maintaining a balance between contending factions, frictions among clerical factions have turned into seemingly non-negotiable divisions. The two sides—those who believe that the system cannot survive without political reform, and those who see reform as a serious blow to the very foundation of the system—are confronting each other in every arena, from the mosques and newspapers to the electoral process. Each side blames the other for the regime's growing crisis of legitimacy.

Saeed Rahnema, Monthly Review, *March 2001.*

have organized both Islamic and secular unions of their own. Despite a wave of newspaper closings and press repression, there are now 22 percent more licensed publications than there were in 1998. Furthermore, journalists have found a new haven in cyberspace beyond the authorities' reach. Currently, more than 1.75 million Iranians reportedly have access to the Internet. Even some nonestablishment ayatollahs have set up their own Web sites to connect with their flock. Their fatwas [decrees] are now used by dissidents to counter the positions of the ruling clerics.

Street demonstrations, labor strikes, teachers' boycotts, and other forms of civil disobedience (such as taunting the morals police with un-Islamic attire) are increasingly common. For instance, thousands of workers demonstrating against poor working conditions managed to increase this year's official minimum wage. Strikes by teachers resulted in a substantial increase in [2003's] education budget. Human rights activists have also pushed the authorities to respond to foreign public opinion. According to the latest report by Human Rights Watch, the Islamic Republic may now start cooperating with foreign monitors for the first time. And in a noteworthy victory, the government shelved a bizarre, religiously sanctioned scheme to set up "temporary weddings" after women's groups, politicians, and some clerics denounced it as legalized prostitution. Most recently, several consecutive days of nationwide student protest in mid-November 2002 forced the supreme leader and the head of the judiciary to order an appeals court to expedite review of the death sentence imposed on reformist scholar Hashem Aghajari. The rahbar also recommended to judges that they avoid opening themselves up to public criticism in their rulings.

Crucial Economic Reforms

The second important change in Iran is a series of small but significant economic measures that are likely to reduce the oligarchs' economic power and help integrate Iran's oil-dependent economy with the global marketplace. The reduction of the hard-liners' financial support is a critical factor in their declining political clout. Indeed, more than any ideological or religious factor, it is control of the nation's economic resources that has allowed Iran's ruling clerics to hold on to power. Donations by devout Muslims, public and private monopolies in key sectors, special business licenses dispensed through patronage, privileged access to cheap credit and foreign exchange, and even widely reported bank fraud have all helped fund the clerics.

Crucial economic reforms, repeatedly promised by [now former president Mohammad] Khatami [since 1998,] have partially taken shape in the last few months. This change has occurred largely in response to pressure from foreign institutions such as the International Monetary Fund, the World Bank, and the European Commission, whose approval is necessary for the government's continued access to foreign credit. Although these reforms will not dry up all the hard-liners' sources of funding overnight, they can affect them in critical areas. For instance, the legalization of private banking and insurance since early 2000 has opened up new venues for the mobilization and allocation of national savings—and removed them from potential political uses by state banks. The government's efforts to consolidate the country's multiple exchange rates since March 2002 has also bottled up corruption stemming from access to cheaper dollars by privileged institutions or favored cronies. Fiscal reform in late 2001 aimed at lowering corporate income taxes and eliminating tax exemption for so-called religious charitable foundations is expected to increase private investment and level the playing field for potential investors. The government's new law to protect foreign investment and enforce some copyrights may reduce dependence on oil revenue. A successful euro bond issue [in the summer of 2002] has opened up another source of foreign exchange to counter volatility in oil prices.

The government has promised to take a number of further steps in the coming months to privatize state enterprises and further diminish the hard-liners' control of the economy. Replacing the inefficient subsidy system (which takes up some 20 percent of GDP [gross domestic product] and benefits mostly the urban rich) with a means-tested social safety net would substantially lighten the government's fiscal burden. In addition, further consolidation of the tax code should reduce the more than 50 different fees that various ministries and agencies impose on production and imports, thus cutting collection costs and special sources of finance for pork-barrel projects. The government's plan to enact a value-added tax in lieu of the current uncollected (and uncollectable) income taxes would likely diminish reliance on oil income and also shrink the bureaucracy.

Replacing the current system of quotas and special licenses on imports with tariffs would eliminate the monopolies enjoyed by politically favored business interests. A comprehensive overhaul of the outdated 1968 commercial code would encourage more transparent and productive ventures, particularly in the small business sector. A revision of the current antibusiness labor law, enacted when leftist ideologues controlled the Fourth Majles in 1990, would encourage new employment. Downsizing the bloated bureaucracy may stop oil income from being invested in politically favored but economically unsound projects. Turning the Tehran Stock Exchange into a self-regulated but politically supervised institution would promote the establishment of mutual funds to attract both domestic and foreign capital.

Finally, Iran's entry into the World Trade Organization [WTO] (so far blocked by the United States) and the conclusion of a comprehensive trade and cooperation accord with the European Union would shake the entrenched economic mafia to its roots and revolutionize the Iranian economy. The WTO's mantra of free markets is anathema to the Islamic Republic's state-dominated and highly politicized economic system. To qualify for full membership, Iran must make a host of economic changes, ranging from trade liberalization to financial deregulation to copyright protection.[3] These new reforms will undoubtedly meet with severe resistance from vested interests. But the urgent need to find jobs for the millions of unemployed—combined with the paucity of domestic investment, sluggish non-oil exports, and weak foreign-exchange reserves—makes turning to the global economy inevitable. And this shift will not be possible without fundamental reform. . . .

3. As of mid-2006, Iran was not a member of the WTO.

A Political Turning Point

The ongoing political impasse, economic distress, and social turmoil . . . all threaten the survival of the Islamic state. The discontent of the Third Force [the youth of Iran] in particular has created a seemingly unstoppable momentum toward change. In its postrevolutionary history, Iran has never been as politically polarized or ideologically divided as it is today. . . .

Threats of mass resignation from members of the Islamic Participation Front (the largest bloc in the Majles), is an ominous warning of a looming constitutional crisis or worse in coming months. Two bills submitted by Khatami to the Majles in September 2002, which are now undergoing the long process of ratification, would curb the veto power of the Council of Guardians and give the president legal authority to force hard-line Islamic courts to abide by the constitution.[4] The renewed crackdown by the judiciary on reformist groups is reported to be an attempt to pressure the president to withdraw these bills. Regardless of the ultimate fate of this controversial legislation, its very introduction marks a major turning point in Iran's domestic political dynamics.

Temporary reversals of democratization nevertheless remain likely. But the Iranian people have sown the seeds of change and the country's theocratic rulers cannot postpone their harvest forever. The autocratic and dubiously Islamic concept of the *velayat-e faqih* is clearly in retreat and the oligarchs know that if they do not bend, they will break.

---

4. The Council of Guardians vetoed both bills.

▌ *"Reformist politicians are out of power."*

Iranian Political Reform Is Faltering

Daniel Tsadik et al.

In the following viewpoint eight prominent scholars and political analysts evaluate the state of the political reform movement in Iran and conclude that the movement is faltering. Reformist politicians are now out of power, and reform is unlikely to occur from within the regime, they point out. They also assert that reformists must understand why their movement got derailed if democratization is ever to occur.

As you read, consider the following questions:

1. What makes Iran both a democracy and a dictatorship, in Menashe Amir's view?

2. Which movement does Bill Samii believe is on its last legs?

3. What is the "China model," as explained by Suzanne Maloney?

Daniel Tsadik et al., "Iran, 25 Years Later: A GLORIA Center Roundtable Discussion," *Middle East Review of International Affairs (MERIA) Journal*, vol. 8, no. 2, June 2004. Copyright GLORIA Center. Reproduced by permission.

Daniel Tsadik: The use of terms like failure and success, as far as I am concerned, don't really provide a better understanding of the situation in Iran. I totally agreed with Dr. [Stephen] Fairbanks in this regard. People in Iran can now talk and say what they think. This is linked to the fact that this revolution came not from the rulers—or, as in Egypt, Syria or Iraq from military officers—but from the people. It was a revolution from below and this makes it a unique phenomenon in the region.

Today, there are fights and tensions, attempts by the conservatives to stop dissent and so on. But the mere fact that there is a struggle and debate—the attempts of many to promote civil society—is an important issue. . . .

Iran Has Failed

Menashe Amir: When I am asked to give a definition of the nature of the Iranian regime I used to say, "This is the most democratic dictatorship and the most dictatorial democracy." Elections in Iran have been a democratic process, but it was a dictatorial one also because of the control over who could run and what they could do afterward. In assessing the twenty-five years of the Iranian regime, I think that they have failed in their three main goals: helping the common people to improve their life; export their revolution; and attract massive popular support within the country. In fact, as Iran failed to export its revolution to Lebanon, Iraq, or Afghanistan, it was in fact the United States which has been more successful at this effort, changing the regime in Afghanistan and Iraq.

In strategic terms, the Iranians are regressing all the time because they have failed to attract the people of other countries and to bring them to support the Iranian revolution. They have also failed to attract Iranian support and today most Iranians want a change of their regime and to overthrow this government. In some cases, they are ready to accept U.S. help in doing so.

Undermining an Election

Barry Rubin: At this point, the interesting question becomes: Why in 2004 did the regime decide to change the system and so undermine the election that the reformist opposition boycotted it. Was it that they thought the ability of reformists to win elections without bringing change was damaging the regime's stability? Or was it that they expected things were going to worsen in the future?

Tom King: To respond briefly, my sense is that the regime took a hard look at the fruits of the reform movement over the previous four years since the 6th Majles [Iran's parliament] was elected and the kinds of manipulations they had to go through to neutralize constantly the reformists' efforts. In particular, I think they saw the statements coming from some of the more radical reformists about changing the nature of the government. They saw that as having some reverberation, particularly that the United States might think that there was in fact a viable opposition and an alternative that could be encouraged from the outside.

In addition, given the U.S. response to the September 11, [2001 terrorist] attacks and the presence of American forces on both Iran's western and eastern borders, in Iraq and Afghanistan, the regime felt pressure closing in. I think they felt that Iran was pretty high on the list that Washington would likely be turning toward as soon as it finished up its business with Baghdad.

There was a combination of two pressures—the internal pressure of the reform movement and the external pressure of regime change rhetoric coming from Washington and actions that seemed to be backing up that rhetoric. I believe that the regime decided that it could not withstand another four years of troublemaking from the legislative branch and that they would risk whatever public reaction might occur in order to avoid that. They were prepared to put down any kind of street

Khatami Lacked the Will to Reform

Far from being on the path of reform and moderation, the Islamic Republic continues to erode the basic human rights of its citizenry. [Then-president Muhammad] Khatami . . . has failed to implement a single substantive reform. On March 17, 2004, he quietly announced that he would no longer seek to push fundamental reform through the Majlis. No amount of negotiation with Khatami, even if he were sincere, would change the fact that he has neither the will nor the power to implement meaningful change.

Michael Rubin, National Review Online, *April 1, 2004.*
www.nationalreview.com.

reaction that may have occurred and they also moved to pre-empt that ahead of time anyway and did it rather effectively actually. Such strong action, I think, was directed from the top and the intent was very clearly to retake control of parliament and reduce these two sources of pressure.

Suzanne Maloney: Let me add that the conservatives risked relatively little by taking the aggressive moves that they did. The population had been so effectively de-politicized over the past four years, particularly since April 2000, and in fact, there were many questions about whether had the conservatives not taken the aggressive approach that they did, would they have done better in the elections than in the past. Given the results of the city council elections last year [2003] in which identifiably reformist candidates did not in fact do very well both because of public disengagement—meaning a refusal to vote—or frustration with the reformists in general.

That is why I get back to this whole idea of freedom being the most important essential good for the revolution to provide. I think clearly the sense you get from talking to average

Iranians is that the most important thing they are looking for in their government is in fact economic progress. While one could question the credibility of this image, the conservatives have at least this image of focusing more intently on the economy. Thus, they were both confident and able to act while, at the same time, were concerned that they could not withstand another four years of reform within the process.

The Reform Movement Is Not Dead

Soli Shahvar: I think the regime knew that it had lost the legitimacy it had in 1979 by the end of the Iran/Iraq war in 1988. That is why it tried to change its image into one of pragmatism and allow the limited liberalism of [President Mohammad] Khatami. But they found that this policy created too many problems for them, like the 1999 and 2003 student revolts and demonstrations. Once they did better in the local elections, this encouraged them to ensure they retook control of the parliament and eventually of the presidency as well.

As for the opposition, it seems that the six years of Khatami and reformism proved to the people that actually there is no hope and no future from the reformist side of the regime, therefore they have given up. In this respect, once the reformist themselves understood the situation, they realized that their only alternative was to boycott the election, a tactic discussed for some time in Iranian opposition circles both inside and outside the country. That was, I would say, one of the only cards open to them and they had to take it. But their deeper problem is what to do now. While reformism is not dead in Iran, the public no longer believes in the promises of the movement [that] so many of them supported [since 1998].

Bill Samii: I agree that the reform movement is not dead. Even before the election, several leading figures in the reformist movement seemed to realize they were going down and what they said is, "This is an opportunity for us when we are out of power to regroup, evaluate where we made mistakes, look forward, and think about how we can serve the people in the future."

I think they genuinely do have to reconsider why the Iranian people have become frankly very cynical about the political process and [why they] see a lot of statements about people saying that, "it is a club in which these elites argue back and forth but don't really get much done." As Dr. Maloney said, when you don't think involvement of politics is going to help you in any way, then economic well-being becomes primary. If you have a family, you have got to support them. If you have got to try to find a job, things like that certainly become really important.

Another reformist member of parliament said basically the same thing. "We have to get back in contact with the people, find out why they are dissatisfied with the reformist movement and then we can advance from there."

Adopting Reformist Rhetoric

Stephen Fairbanks: Reformist politicians are out of power but that doesn't mean that reformism itself has come to an end. Also, many of the politicians labeled as conservative have adopted a lot of the reformist rhetoric as far as also advocating increased democracy. Whether that is really going to happen or not, I am not going to predict. But the conservatives themselves are tremendously divided between the very hardline ones that we think of most often and quite a number of others [who are] more technocratic [and] who want to bring about economic reforms in a way that the reformist politicians were never able to do and who also talk about much more democratic reform, including establishing stronger political parties which appeal more to the people.

I would also point out as far as whether the revolution has been a failure or not, the situation of the provinces to which this regime over the years has devoted much more attention than I think the monarchy ever did. In terms of economic development of the rural areas, it brought water and electrification and inroads and other improvements to their lives. I think we see that reflected in the rural areas' voting statistics which have in recent years given stronger support for the regime in the rural areas because of the economic benefits that they have been getting.

Bill Samii: One movement that probably is on its last legs is the Islamic Participation Front, basically created for Khatami. It was created in late 1998 or early 1999 and since that time has basically become more and more radicalized. In contrast, the Mujahadin of the Islamic Revolution Organization—not the group based in Iraq but the reformist movement within Iran—seems to have more staying power, with some serious political activists involved. . . .

The Regime's Response

Daniel Tsadik: Even if indeed reformist movements were weakened, and this is probably the case, there is still a need for reforms, including such economic problems as unemployment, etc., etc. I will raise a question: "Do you think the regime itself will pursue these reforms, give them some kind of Islamic garb and some Islamic symbols, thus actually pursuing some of the reformist agenda, which previously was led by the reformist movements?"

Soli Shahvar: The hardliners claim that the reformists have failed and that they will improve the Iranian economy, to succeed where the reformists have failed in solving Iran's problems.

Suzanne Maloney: I think what was just referred to is the idea of a "China model" that would let the conservatives push for economic reforms while maintaining some degree of political orthodoxy and probably a certain amount of cultural liberalization or at least social tolerance of greater freedom on the streets in order to preserve their own basis of credibility and legitimacy. I think that this government—and frankly any Iranian regime—is going to have a very difficult time in actually implementing those reforms. . . .

I would probably be the one person here to actually declare the Reform Movement to some extent dead and that is not so much the movement but the paradigm of reform from within, change of the institutions that Dr. Rubin and Dr. Samii described so effectively. The idea that these institutions can be changed by the institutions of the government themselves I think is no longer valid in the current power structure of Iran. The reformist parliament made great efforts to take on the Council of Guardians by attempting to address its spiraling budget and trying to create trouble for some of the now hardline nominations back in 2001 and take some of these other steps along with the twin bills which would have addressed the Council of Guardian's power to actually vet candidates.

Clearly, they failed in all of those regards and now they are out of power. I think to some extent the whole idea that the government could change itself from within was a hopeful one and might have worked had the reformists addressed their task in a slightly more aggressive way and used their popular mandate. That clearly now is no longer valid. I guess for me the question is really, "Will the reformists be able to successfully push for change from outside the system itself?" To me that really comes down to, "Will they be able to—or will they be willing to—push for the idea of referendum," which I think has a certain degree of popularity on the Iranian street.

> *"Almost every young Iranian has a political opinion."*

Iranian Youths Will Work for Reform

Golnar Motevalli

Iran is a young nation, with more than two-thirds of its population age thirty or younger. In the following viewpoint Golnar Motevalli asserts that Iranian youth are an important political force that cannot be ignored by the nation's government. Motevalli asserts that young Iranians are knowledgeable about Western culture and are eager to live lives that are free from traditional Islamic restrictions. At the same time, Motevalli contends, young Iranians are proud of their cultural heritage, a stance that must be balanced with their admiration of Western norms. Motevalli is a journalist who has been published in periodicals such as Middle East *and* New Statesman.

As you read, consider the following questions:

1. Why does Maryam, as cited by the author, believe her life is becoming easier?

2. How do young Iranians view the 2003 war in Iraq, according to Motevalli?

Golnar Motevalli, "The Changing Face of Iran," *Middle East*, March 2003, p. 56. Reproduced by permission.

3. In the author's opinion, what has been the consequence of Iran's high standards of education?

With 69% of Iran's population under the age of 30, the traditional, Islamic parliamentary elites are acutely aware of the potential political dynamism of these upcoming generations. Most young and educated Iranians are keen to emulate western fashions, but reconciling such desires with the social responsibilities required by a life under an Islamic political system can often be frustrating. Reza is a 20-year-old student of veterinary medicine. He lives with his family in an affluent area of Tehran. "Most young people voted for [now former president] Khatami, but those who did are now unhappy with him," he observes. Although Reza was not old enough to vote in 1997, the year Mohammed Khatami was elected to power, newspaper articles and cuttings of the President's rise to power are still tacked to his bedroom walls. As he explains: "Those are there as a reminder of how naive I once was—Khatami is all talk and no action. He promised so many things and delivered little in return."

Reza's 17-year-old sister, Maryam, agrees but also feels that her life is gradually getting easier. "I can be free in school to question my beliefs; education is more open-minded, particularly to western concepts. For instance, we are taught Aristotle, [Friedrich] Nietzsche and [Emile] Durkheim at secondary school and encouraged to apply their theories to Islamic philosophy. It is also easier to access information since the Internet came here."

A More Relaxed Climate

Like anywhere else in the world, the impact of the Internet on the daily life of many Iranians has been profound. It is the only completely uncensored medium of information available to the public, and as a result young Iranians can freely view western websites containing information on issues ranging from politics to Picasso, Shakespeare to Shakira. It has also become a playground to meet and socialize. Levels of social and sexual restraint upon Iran's youth are notably high; Internet chat rooms provide an outlet for young people feeling stressed by the laws and social mores that govern their lives.

The increasingly relaxed and liberal political climate manifests itself in obvious ways in Tehran: overcoats are getting shorter, thinner, lighter and tighter; open-toed shoes and painted nails—as well as a lot of make-up—are no longer an exception for girls and young women. However, such changes are not representative of Iranian society as a whole. Kaaveh, who is 24, lives in Esfahan. Arguably Iran's most beautiful city, it is an immaculately well-kept tourist attraction. He feels the climate of control has strengthened to a ridiculous degree: "Where you see young people in Tehran enjoying greater freedom, here it has become worse, they're making up here for whatever control is lacking in Tehran. . . . Undercover Islamic informers [Commiteh] are now easy to recognise and they're everywhere". Kaaveh has many a tale to tell of how friends have suffered at the hands of this strict control: "some of my friends have been approached by the Commiteh . . . and told-off for wearing the wrong clothes. It happens a lot in this city," he confirms.

"Increased freedom has also widened the gap between rich and poor," says Kaaveh, and this is visible across Iran. It is now easier for rich Iranian families to show off their wealth because western goods are more readily available. The wealthy enjoy holidays to Dubai, satellite TV and four-wheel-drive cars, whilst the poorest families continue to exist close to the breadline as they have pretty much since the revolution. Kaaveh feels the Iranian government is to blame. He feels that too much money is being spent outside Iran, that charity should begin at home. "They keep giving money to causes which have nothing to do with Iran. We can't afford that and I don't support it."

Cox & Forkum. Reproduced by permission.

A Growing Political Voice

In contrast to the West, almost every young Iranian has a political opinion. The [2003] US attack on Iraq is a hot issue for many. Young people are overwhelmingly against military action. The older generations, who clearly remember the Iran-Iraq war, show more diversity in their opinions—from the belief that it's an imperialist, western and purely economic enterprise, to the idea that Iran should not align herself with Iraq. In response to a speech by President Khatami [in early 2003], in which he referred to [former Iraqi leader] Saddam Hussein as his "brother," a reformist newspaper subsequently carried the headline, "How is your 'Brother', Mr Khatami? Have you forgiven him for killing thousands of young Iranians?"

A collective political voice which expresses the desire to see Iran become an independent political, social, cultural and economic entity, is growing increasingly powerful. Many want to see the country ridding itself of alliances with countries, such as Iraq, that have left a violent and painful stain on the country's history. High standards of education within the country have resulted in a large section of the community—particularly the literate and university-educated—having a keen interest in politics, sociology and issues which stimulate a satisfying degree of intellectual discussion. Young Iranians, however, chiefly express a desire to live free, relaxed and liberal lives. They want the autonomy of choice to dress in a western style if they wish, whilst maintaining their own unique sense of Persian identity.

When questioned over the quality of their 'Persian-ness', they are unambiguous in steadfastly defending their national identity and cultural heritage. Such displays of pride in political and religious history, however, sometimes sit uneasily alongside desires of aspiring to western norms. Iran's government has high hopes for future generations and there has always been an emphasis on rewarding young high achievers: academic award ceremonies are enthusiastically publicised through the general media and are an important part of public life. Therefore, it has become important for the Iranian government to ensure that it knows in exactly which direction these 'new Iranians' will take the legacy of the Islamic revolution.

> "[Young Iranians] have turned inward,
> settling for the opportunity to make a
> little more money and have a little
> more fun."

Iranian Youths Will Not
Soon Work for Reform

Azadeh Moaveni

*In the following viewpoint Azadeh Moaveni claims that young
men and women in Iran have given up on political reform and
have instead invested their energies in partying and buying fashionable clothes. She argues that the Iranian government has
loosened laws governing behavior in order to keep youths content, thereby avoiding political unrest. However, Moaveni cautions that despite this temporary diversion, youths will one day
rise in protest of the repressive Iranian state. Moaveni is the
Tehran correspondent for* Time *magazine and the author of* Lipstick Jihad: A Memoir of Growing Up Iranian in America and
American in Iran.

As you read, consider the following questions:

1. How did Iran's ruling clerics first respond to being labeled part of the "axis of evil," according to the author?

Azadeh Moaveni, "Fast Times in Tehran," *Time*, June 13, 2005, p. 38. Copyright ©
2005 Time, Inc. All rights reserved. Reprinted by permission.

2. Why does Moaveni label Laleh Seddigh's life a "win-win situation?"

3. Why does the author doubt that U.S.-sponsored regime change will occur in Iran?

On my first night back in Tehran, I met some friends for drinks. It was a hazy night, and we convened at an intersection of a major expressway. I assumed we would head to someone's house, but my friends had something else in mind. In four cars, we took off down the highway, going 60 miles an hour, swerving to get close enough so I could pass a cocktail made of whiskey with mulberry nectar out the passenger-side window of our Korean hatchback to a friend in one of the other cars. Our stereo screeched Shaggy's Hey Sexy Lady; theirs, insipid Lebanese pop. Tehran, with its murals of suicide bombers, Versace billboards and rickety buses adorned with portraits of Shi'ite saints, slid by in a smoggy blur. We careered past police, who didn't blink. The driver of my car frowned as I flung out my arm to grab another drink. "You can't do this properly," she said, "if you keep closing your eyes."

In today's Tehran, a land where political expression can be lethal and thrills hard to come by, dangerous pastimes have a special appeal. Young people are constantly drawn to activities that are extraordinarily outrageous—and very now. When we tired of the bar on wheels, we stopped at a pomegranate-juice stand that stays open until 4 a.m. for anyone who needs a late fix. "Sorbet? Juice? Something else?" asked the juiceman, arching a brow. Ecstasy, the leisure drug of elite Iranians, used to be smuggled into Iran from Europe. Now garage chemists produce the tablets locally, and a hit costs about $2. I slunk low in the car seat and muttered to my Iranian friend, "Aren't we too old for this?" What I really wanted to ask was, When will you stop considering this freedom? When will you care again about what's happening in the world?

Buying Off Iran's Youth

When I left Tehran in 2002, after spending two years in the country my parents had left behind in the 1970s for the U.S., life was different. In many ways it was worse. After the U.S. Administration declared Iran part of an "axis of evil," the ruling clerics lashed out at home, enforcing social strictures with such vigor that we wouldn't leave parties without first chewing several pieces of gum to conceal the alcohol on our breath, in case we encountered a checkpoint run by Islamic paramilitaries. When the rhetoric cooled, the system turned its sights back to its angry young people and essentially decided to stanch their discontent by buying them off. While continuing to brutally suppress all political dissent, the mullahs boosted subsidies on gas and household commodities. But most significant, they began loosening control over the lifestyle choices of the 48 million Iranians under the age of 30, who make up more than two-thirds of the population.

Judging by what I saw on a 10-day trip to Iran [in May 2005], the strategy has worked. Today young Iranians despair of political change. Resigned to the rule of autocratic mullahs, they have turned inward, settling for the opportunity to make a little more money and have a little more fun. Gone are dreams of [Cuban revolutionary] Che Guevara and a quick, painless revolution, replaced by the allure of pyramid schemes and cheap trips to India. Although it's too late to buy the love of Iran's youth, the mullahs seem happy to settle for torpor. "You have a situation," says my friend Karim Sadjadpour, an analyst in Tehran for the International Crisis Group, "where the majority of Iranians have neither the luxury to risk their livelihoods waging political protest nor the nothing-to-lose desperation and rage that result from penury."

The great buy-off may prove to be a temporary fix, given that the government's beneficence is tied to surplus funds engendered by high oil prices. Polls show that 50% of Iranians plan to vote in [June 2005's] presidential election, compared

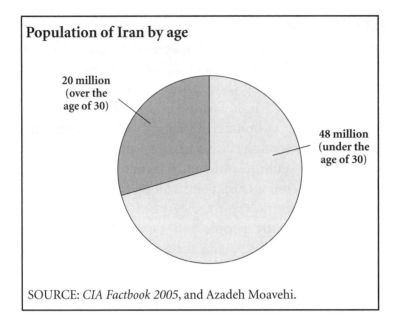

Population of Iran by age

20 million
(over the
age of 30)

48 million
(under the
age of 30)

SOURCE: *CIA Factbook 2005*, and Azadeh Moavehi.

with 66% in 2001. Lower turnout matters in a system that cares about public opinion, but that has long stopped being a concern of the Islamic republic. The regime is cunning enough to dispense new social liberties carefully, with periodic perfunctory raids reminding young people that they are being given freedom and shouldn't confuse it with a right or an accomplishment. But young Iranians probably can't be bought off indefinitely. The hedonism and greed of the moment mask a profound frustration that could still boil over. The question is, Will anyone notice until it does?

Relaxed Moves

The day after surviving the cocktail hour from hell, I attended a practice session of 127, Iran's hottest underground rock band. Because the regime still pretends to oppose the toxic culture of the West, rock music is semi-taboo, so the band rehearses in a soundproof bunker inside an abandoned greenhouse in a low-rise complex of concrete apartment blocks on the outskirts of the city. The band members compare themselves with writers in Soviet Russia—miserably creative, creatively miserable. They sing in English and dress in the uniform of global grunge: long sideburns, faded Converse sneakers and plaid shirts. The band is beloved by young Iranians because its music communicates a despair that has few avenues for expression.

For my benefit they play *My Sweet Little Terrorist Song*, a sly lament about Iran's inclusion in President George W. Bush's "axis of evil": "I just wanna watch Dylan live./ I won't fly into the Pentagon alive." Some of their songs can be read as cries for political change, but like everything else here, they are ambiguous enough to be easily defendable in a courtroom, should it come to that. As I sat in 127's practice bunker, I caught myself wondering, Where were you when I lived here? As recently as three years ago, it was still somewhat risque to turn music up really loud or wear Capri pants in certain parts of town. Now music like 127's, which offers an artful expression of a dark, complex reality, helps make living in Iran more bearable. Even the murals around Tehran of scowling ayatollahs have been repainted to give them toothy smiles.

The social mores are relaxed enough to accommodate even women like Laleh Seddigh, 28, a race-car driver who is the Iranian version of Danica Patrick. Seddigh wears bright pink veils, designer sunglasses and has won a race or two on Iran's racing circuit. State television has refused to broadcast her standing on the podium to receive her prize, but that has allowed Seddigh—in the manner of 127—to protect her radical chic. It's a win-win arrangement: she gets her fast cars and fast lifestyle, and the regime gets a poster girl for its new tolerance. "Women haven't gone after many of their rights here," she tells me. "If they pursue them, so much is possible." She pauses, perhaps realizing she sounds like one of the regime's chador-clad apologists. "Not that it's easy."

Life Seems Better

Ten years ago, the cultural and material poverty of life in Iran would have sent a privileged young woman like her fleeing to

London or Los Angeles. Today Seddigh drives a silver BMW, drinks authentic Red Bull, wears Puma shoes and travels regularly to Europe. Her middle-class friends can afford real Coca-Cola as well as trips to Goa [India] and Malaysia. (It's generally cheaper to travel east.) They meet friends online through the networking website Orkut.com and feel connected through the things they buy, the Internet they're addicted to and their ability to travel to a global community larger than their own. Will they vote? Mostly no. Do they despise the Islamic republic? Pretty much. But their inclination to do anything about it has never been so weak and the distractions never so plentiful. It's easier to lower your expectations when the only life you have known seems to be getting better.

The main reason for that improvement is simple. Thanks to soaring oil prices, there is plenty of money sloshing around. On a Saturday afternoon, I went to lunch at the gleaming kabob palace Nayeb, which is where you go in Tehran to see and be seen—while eating lots of grilled meat. The prices had tripled in my absence, and so had the line for a table. As we wait, I chat with a waiter named Vali Joodi, who tells me he wakes up at 5 a.m. each day to commute from the working-class suburb of Shahriar. Four years ago, he asked his girlfriend to marry him. Once he started tallying what they would need for rent, food and a ceremony, however, he realized he didn't earn enough to support two. Then he discovered that the government offers low-interest marriage loans that can be paid back over a long period. Billboards in Tehran advertise various forms of government loans, all with low interest rates. Agricultural loans go for 11% interest and can be invested in a bank for an 18% return.

Those sorts of handouts buy the state grudging acquiescence even from low-income workers like Joodi. When he married in 2001, the loan was $700; today it's approaching $1,300. Joodi is far from content. He tells me, "I work from 6 a.m. to midnight, come home exhausted and see my family for half an hour before I pass out." But the loan clearly mattered in his life, allowing him to marry at once, which could mean the difference between his continuing to tolerate the Islamic system and revolting against it.

Suppression Still Occurs

Of course, the mullahs still resort to heavy-handed means of suppressing disgruntlement. About two years ago, I watched as an unmarked Iranian Paykan drove up to the curb outside a meeting of student activists. Plainclothes agents of the hardline judiciary jumped out and dived at the organizers standing outside. In broad daylight, in front of journalists, the agents dragged the students along the ground, tearing their clothes and bloodying their faces. The agents dumped the activists in an idling car and then peeled away. It took about five minutes for the students to disappear into the recesses of the system. On this trip, I went to a fashionable cafe to see Amir Balali, a former student activist who had spent time in prison for his organizing. In the middle of the afternoon, young couples are bent over banana splits while the speakers purr French lounge music. Balali, 25, is an urbane young man wearing an Umbro shirt and jeans and carrying a Nokia digital camera phone. In 2002 he was arrested. While in prison, he says, he was kept standing—sleepless, facing a wall—for 72 hours straight and was beaten.

Balali describes Iranian society as "an utter catastrophe" and explains that his peers have become used to behaving as though the unresponsive regime doesn't exist, bypassing it entirely to solve their problems. He considered organizing a protest around a candidate for next week's election but then realized that no one was particularly worked up, including him. "No one is interested in coalescing around anything beyond themselves," he says with a shrug. "Their idols aren't Che Guevara anymore. They're Bill Gates and Angelina Jolie." He predicts that the Islamic republic will eventually crumble and that change here will be chaotic and painful. "The lawful, peaceful approach didn't work," says Balali. "Young people can only tolerate this for so long."

When you try to view the future through the eyes of a young Iranian, it seems clear that there is no easy route to a new Iran. The government of outgoing President Mohammed Khatami initially raised hopes for political change but didn't deliver. For many young Iranians fed up with clerical rule, the possibility of U.S.-sponsored regime change in Iran once offered the distant hope of a simple and quick solution, but with an insurgency boiling next door in Iraq, it's now clear that that would be neither a solution nor pain-free.

*"Iran cannot forever claim that its back-
wardness is due to the machinations of
others to keep them behind."*

Iranians Must Take Responsibility for Their Future

Reza Pahlavi

*Iranians must stop allowing themselves to be victimized by do-
mestic and foreign forces and take a larger role in shaping the
future of their nation, Reza Pahlavi contends in the following
viewpoint. He argues that a new Iran must be one that is no
longer ruled by a theocratic government and which normalizes
relationships with other nations and the international business
community. Pahlavi concludes that such changes cannot occur
unless Iranians demand a voice in policy making and stop blam-
ing their problems on other people. Pahlavi is the son of Muhammad Reza Pahlavi, the former shah, or king, of Iran, who
was deposed following the revolution in 1979 that established
Iran as an Islamic theocracy.*

Reza Pahlavi, *Winds of Change: The Future of Democracy in Iran*. Washington, DC:
Regnery Publishing, 2002. Copyright © 2002 Henry Regnery Company. All rights re-
served. Reproduced by special permission of Regnery Publishing, Inc., Washington,
D.C.

As you read, consider the following questions:

1. How did the role of clerics change after 1979, according to Pahlavi?
2. In the author's view why is normalization a concern of the international business community?
3. In Pahlavi's opinion what does Japan exemplify?

Since the advent of Islam, our clergymen have served as a moral compass. Spirituality has been an inseparable part of our culture. And our men of the cloth have been respected by the various sectors of our society.

But the advent of an Islamic theocracy in 1979 introduced a totally different role of religion and clergy. For the first time, these revolutionary clerics stepped out of the mosques and entered the political arena. Rather than being moral advisers to society, they became the decision makers and attempted to manage the daily affairs of the country. Even worse, they attempted to rewrite our history, our culture, and our traditions.

Soon, the once revered clergy had to provide daily answers to the most difficult social, economic, and policy questions. When their answers fell short, so did reverence to[ward] them.

Today, moral guidance has been replaced by clerical censorship and dictatorial fiat. Daily, the ruling clerics in Tehran pass judgments on which newspapers should be allowed and which banned, what type of clothing is appropriate and what is not, what music will be allowed and what will not. The sad fact is that clerical policies have generated a great deal of animosity and resentment—an immense disservice to our religious heritage.

The dramatic consequence of the Islamic revolution has been the realization that theocracy is an unacceptable form of government. Iranians, among them an increasing number of highly intellectual and vocal clergymen, are openly debating the merits of secularism—a clear separation of religion from government.

This growing number of clerics and religious intellectuals see no contradiction between modernity and Islam. More importantly, progressive theologians do not see democracy as a direct threat to religion. In fact, the debate in Iran over religion in recent years has been among the most advanced and thought provoking in the entire Muslim world. This advanced thinking is the result of the obvious shortcomings of a religiously based government.

It is critically important, however, to clarify that the rejection of theocracy—of an Islamic republic—does not, in anyway, mean a rejection of Islam. Equally important, separation of religion and state does not only restrict the clergy from interfering in government affairs, but the government from interfering in religion.

Like so many other Muslim countries, Iran faces the dilemma of what to do about calls for Family Law—for example, issues pertaining to divorce procedures and a women's rights to inheritance—which is exclusively based on the Shari'a, the Islamic Law based on the Quran and the Hadith. However, if democracy—representative government—is the order of the day, then these laws must be based on popular will. That being the case, the Shari'a may have an influence over the language of such civil laws, if so wished by the people. The specifics and implementation of these principles should be left to the future constitution, which will need to be drafted and approved by the people of Iran.

Thus I hope to see an end to theocracy, and the separation of religion from government as being in the best interest of Islam and democracy. As outlined above, it would present a unique opportunity for those in the regime to exit politics peacefully.

Normalization Will Benefit Iran

Why do I advocate dialogue and normalization of relations between the U.S. and Iran, even though the lack of democracy and individual freedom and the widespread violations of human rights, particularly women's rights in Iran have forced scholars like myself to exile or migration? . . .

I believe any positive and conciliatory overture on the side of the U.S. toward normalization of the relations between Iran and the U.S. will serve not only the normalization of Iran's foreign policy, but also the normalization of politics in Iran as a whole. It will serve Iran's move to a post-revolutionary state of institutionalization and stabilization.

Nayereh Tohidi, speech at the Symposium on U.S.-Iran Relations,
November 1997.

Seventh, concerning the normalization of international relations, I boldly favor—if certain preconditions are met by the current regime, especially concerning human rights, the media, and the liberation of political prisoners—the restitution of such relations as soon as possible. This will remove unnecessary burdens on the people of Iran. In addition, history clearly demonstrates that totalitarian systems break down faster when there is dialog and openness. The rulers can no longer hide behind walls of isolation, unquestioned and unexamined. Democracy demands that leaders be accountable to their people. This is precisely why many hard-liners in Iran seek to block normalization of diplomatic relations with the West.

Normalization and dialog are not just the concern of governments, but of the international business community as well. As part of this policy, international businesses will naturally be at the forefront of reengagement with Iran. However, such efforts must be conducted with the long-term interests of the Iranian people in mind: the pursuit of business interest must not be at the expense of human interest.

Eighth, I call strongly for civic responsibility. Today's problems require the active participation of our people. In this respect, Iranians need to take much more responsibility than before. Traditionally, we have had the tendency to rely overly on powerful leaders to make all the decisions and take all the initiatives. By the same token, we as a people have tended to blame foreign influence and conspiracies for our ills. In short, "victimization" at the hand of domestic or foreign forces has been our favorite cultural lament.

How long are we going to blame our misfortunes on others? When do we take responsibility ourselves? Clearly, that cannot happen until people are given a chance to take responsibility. When they are denied it, they feel frustrated and never develop a civic sense. The curse of our history is that the public has never been able to participate in a politically meaningful way in the system. As a result, we have often felt either helpless or alienated. That mentality was prevalent in my father's era and continues today.

Iran cannot forever claim that its backwardness is due to the machinations of others to keep them behind. We need to step up and demand a voice in policymaking, offer ideas, corrections, and accept the consequences. No person or system can afford people happiness or success without personal responsibility.

Today, I sense that the era of conspiracy theory, "victimization," is being replaced by a new era of modern thinking and self-realization. Our people have awakened. They have paid a heavy price to learn the merits of democracy. Our youth are, on a daily basis, pushing the envelope in their quest for self-empowerment. My call for civic duty is embedded in my profound desire to ensure that the old psyche be forever abandoned and replaced by a new sense of national pride in self-determination and rule.

My final point involves the controversial issue of the impact of Western culture on Iranian life. Indeed, this topic has been at the center of a heated debate in our country in recent decades. It is controversial because, despite the many positives the West has to offer, there are negatives as well. Among its greatest contributions are the principles of democracy, individual liberty, and human rights, which are compatible with all cultures and civilizations. However, differing values held by Eastern and Western cultures continue to fuel a debate about which aspects to choose and which to leave behind. Japan is one of the better examples of how Eastern societies can embrace the best of the West while preserving their own value systems.

Similarly, with a heritage that spans millennia, Iran is perfectly capable of preserving its cultural identity and value system while choosing the best of Western ideals. Interestingly, it is often forgotten that the best of Western ideals, such as human rights, pluralism, tolerance, and inclusion of ethnic and religious minorities, are deeply rooted in our culture.

Since its emergence, and in order to suppress demands for political liberalization, the clerical regime has mislabeled the debate, asking the people to choose between "West-toxication" and national/cultural independence.

It is one thing to advocate a rejection of foreign interference in our country's domestic affairs: no patriotic Iranian could argue with that. The issue, however, is not compromising our cultural identity: it is the mechanism by which we can attain real modernization, both politically and economically. We need not become in the least "West-toxicated" in order to succeed. In other words, modernization need not automatically mean Westernization. Clearly, we can build our own Iranian experience with a forward-looking attitude and modern thought, and without alienating the rest of the world in the process.

> *"Iran's economy has been facing horrendous problems caused by the mullahs' ill-advised economical policies."*

Iran Faces a Perilous Economic Future

Vahid Isabeigi

In the following viewpoint Vahid Isabeigi argues that the greed of Iran's religious clerics, or mullahs, has caused the nation's economy to decline. According to Isabeigi, these high-ranking clerics control 70 percent of Iran's wealth and seek to prevent economic competition by thwarting the development of the private sector. Consequently, Isabeigi maintains, ordinary Iranians have become poorer and lack access to well-made products, unless they can find goods on the black market. At the time this viewpoint was written, Isabeigi was an Iranian student who was studying engineering in Canada.

As you read, consider the following questions:

1. According to the author, how much poorer has the average Iranian become since the Islamic Revolution?

2. As explained by Isabeigi, why are there no private automobile manufacturers in Iran?

Vahid Isabeigi, "Iran's Plundered Future," http://www.payvand.com, October 1, 2003. Reproduced by permission.

3. In the author's view why has Iran failed to reduce its dependence on petroleum?

[T]wenty-four] years after the outbreak of the revolution, ... trends exhibit how Iran's economy, thanks to outrageous ravages by mullahs [Muslim religious clerics], has deteriorated to such extents that even if the best economical schemes were employed overnight, the impacts of their [the mullahs'] mismanagement are likely to reverberate for decades to come. Clerics, while having repeatedly declared their support for the society's neglected spectrum, have concocted a bizarre capitalism addressing their own ilk which doesn't have any resemblance to any internationally-accepted system. This corrupt system, which has caused an average Iranian to get 7% poorer as opposed to [the system in] pre-revolutionary Iran, has substantially taken its toll on Iranians.

Over this lengthy stretch of time, the *bonyads*, the so-called Foundations of the Oppressed, each of which is operated by a well-to-do mullah, have been hoisted to a level where they have the final say over the economical policies of the country. Having pocketed a considerable amount of the country's wealth, these *bonyads* constitute the prime reason for the spread of corruption, which has turned into one of the most intractable economical and social glitches the country is plagued with. In fact, if it hadn't been for these *bonyads*, which form the backbone of the regime and which, contemporaneously, are founded with the money pinched from ordinary Iranians who are forced to contribute huge sums of money to these organisations, the economy could have seen signs of improvement.

Two Economic Facades

In order to fathom the basic structure of the Iranian economy, it should be reminded that the economy of Iran appears under two different facades. One facade is the one which is under the hegemony of the moderates and which is supposed to cater for ordinary people of all walks. Compared with the second guise, not much budget is allocated to this one. This branch encompasses basic services employing millions (namely the majority of the working population) of not-necessarily-very-devout people. These people are comprised of teachers, majority of state employees, and workers, all of whom have borne the brunt of the state's outrageous economical mismanagement. The second and less conspicuous facade of the Iranian economy is the one controlled by the *bonyads* which are dominant on automobile production, the extraction of the country's petroleum, hotels, banks, shipment companies, and many other vital industries.

According to a ... news item by IRNA [Islamic Republic News Agency], 70% of the country's immense wealth is controlled by these 3000 hard-liners, all of whom have grown immeasurably wealthy. That is why the majority of the country's population of 65 million people, who are only permitted to control 30% of the wealth, have been suffering from the lack of [the] most indispensable food products. In fact, the consumption of meat, due to the inability of millions of people to afford it, has plummeted substantially. Iranian cities are nowadays home to hundreds of thousands of street children and mendicants with a tendency towards increasing. As is apparent, just as in the state structure of Iran, Iran has two economies. This, in other words, signifies that in Iran there exists a state within a state.

The Private Sector Struggles

While the monopoly of the wealthy mullahs on [the] economy in Iran has precipitated a weird sort of capitalism to take form, the tolerance of these foregoing invincible rulers of 3000 mullahs to the emergence of private sector is inexplicably low. The development of [the] private sector, despite the perseverance of people engaged in this sector, has for decades been stunted and discouraged. What does really scourge the mullahs about the possible emergence of a viable private sector? Why are the hard-liners so opposed to laissez-faire? After all, [the] Islamic Republic bears no resemblance to any communist state where the wealth is supposedly distributed equally amongst all the members of the society. Neither does its moribund economy look like that of a social republic or a pure capitalist state. Given all these yardsticks, what forms the source of [the] mullahs' contempt for the emergence of a private sector? The answer is very facile: greed. Since the *bonyads* operated by these personages are dominant on the country's major industrial facilities, the clerics are diametrically opposed to the emergence of strong competitors operating in the realm of the industries they control since they are well aware that in an atmosphere of competition, due to their abysmal service and the low quality of the products they manufacture, they would be vanquished miserably in the presence of their private competitors.

The existing private competitors are hardly capable of surviving (with a myriad of them going bankrupt every year) while being constantly harassed in a bid of the state to incapacitate them. For instance, why isn't a single private automobile manufacturing company allowed to exist in Iran? The answer is very simple: The affluent mullahs who own automobile factories do not want to confront the hassle of having to produce higher quality cars in order to compete with their potential rivals. That is why, despite the ineffably low quality of cars manufactured within the country, Iran today is one of the most expensive places on earth in terms of the prices of cars. That is why, shabby Paykaans, built after [the] 1960 model English Helmand and still possessing exactly the same qualities, cost around $7,500. The clerics, due to their lack of skills in the field of industry and also to their disinclination, find it appropriate that ordinary Iranians ride in 1960-style junks even at indescribably jolting prices while they themselves can

Deteriorating Conditions

The economic conditions of Iran's working class have been dreadfully deteriorating in the past few years. A solid majority of people in Iran now live in poverty. There is unprecedented massive unemployment and underemployment. Unemployment among youth, the highest percentage of Iran's population, and women is exceedingly high. The largest part of [the] working class is not covered by unemployment insurance benefits, and for those eligible it is below the poverty line and does not get enforced properly. Average wages are significantly lower than the average costs of living.

International Alliance in Support of Workers in Iran,
"Iranian Workers Fight Back! Support Their Demands!" 2003.

make billions of dollars by thwarting the development of private enterprise thus augmenting their sway on the Iranian economy. This despite the fact that the poorly-produced automobiles on Iran's roads have been blamed to be amongst the main instigators of hundreds of thousands of accidents claiming thousands of lives annually.

The same propensity is evident in the suffering and almost non-existent tourism sector of the country as well. It is amazing that along with cars and other industrial goods, the country's all-luxurious hotels belong to any of these 3000 mullahs, who, owing to their sheer inexperience to run such facilities, have seriously caused the number of customers to decline while turning down any entrepreneur intending to construct posh hotels or tourism facilities since this would be deleterious to their own business. In other words, ordinary people are bearing the brunt of the mullahs' inexperience who, while dominating the sector, don't even allow a single competitor to emerge. Privatisation, which was prescribed by a few reformist politicians as the only cure to Iran's ailing economy, has frequently been impeded. In fact, the country's popularly elected but powerless [now former] president, [Muhammad] Khatami, has many times expressed his dejection of the lack of ample privatisation.

Dependence on Petroleum

The same attitude of these powerful and affluent mullahs owning *bonyads* is very prominent in the backbone of the Iranian economy, i.e., the petroleum sector. For more than two decades, on account of inadvisable policies with respect to the extraction, production, and consumption of petroleum along with the foregoing restrictions imposed on [the] private sector, Iran's economy has never been permitted to reduce its enduring dependence on this product (as is evident from the fact that more than 80% of the export revenues are earned from petroleum). While public access to the management of [the] petroleum industry is strictly forbidden by these well-to-do mullahs, the lack of knowledge evinced by these clerics to properly run this branch of industry has shown its adverse and preposterous outcomes. Due to the dilapidated state of the refineries in Iran, the petrol [gasoline] produced within the country has an inconceivably low quality. This poses two very pernicious long-term consequences for the country: Firstly, it causes the low-quality (but somehow overpriced) domestically-produced automobiles to break down quite easily, thus causing hundreds of dollars of damage to the engine of the car purchased by the owner. Secondly, and foremost, the low quality of domestically-produced cars along with the poor quality of Iran's petrol, thanks to the decrepit state of the refineries, have given rise to Tehran's infamous air pollution, a problem that has reached such acute levels that Tehran's air is conceived as one of the lowest quality in the world. Apart from Tehran, other growing cities have started to experience this insurmountable problem. These are all attributable to the fact that the clerics are unwilling to relinquish the assets they have seized and are reluctant to ... improve these sectors [or] let the private sector step in. The very same trend is also noticeable in the exports of the country. Why doesn't Iran export a significant amount of industrial items (if ever it does)? The answer is, the plight of Iran's industry is so wretched that not many third world countries would think about importing the low-quality industrial items produced by Iran. In this case, what do the mullahs in charge resort to? Very simple: they seek to sell them to their own people [for] incredibly high prices to compensate for the damage while strictly blocking the legal entrance of higher quality foreign goods.

Given these strict conditions and appalling quality of domestically produced industrial goods, many Iranians who are stultified with this status quo are virtually, if not explicitly, compelled by the state to illegally import foreign-made, higher quality, and more affordable items such as electronic goods, which are widely available on the other side of the Persian Gulf. Yet, the clerics in Iran, who lag behind when it comes to handling the mammoth task of adapting the Iranian industry to that of the modern world, have not missed the opportunity to avidly partake in the smuggling business. In fact, many dockyards on the Iranian side of the Persian Gulf are operated by Agha-Zadehs [corrupt officials], who engage very actively in smuggling billions-[of]-dollars-worth [of] tax-free goods into the country.

Other Nations Are Surpassing Iran

What is more, the grave conditions of economy and the Iranian industry divulge a highly bizarre trend: Most Asian countries that were economically less advanced than Iran, have, thanks to their decisive efforts, now greatly surpassed Iran in various aspects. South Korea, which is defined as the emerging industrial empire of the Asian continent, has moved from the position of a struggling economy into one of the world's leading industrial powers. It should be noted that until 1979, the GDP [gross domestic product] per capita in South Korea was lower than that of Iran. At present, South Korea is one of the major trading partners of Iran engaging in billions-of-dollars-worth [of] investments. Furthermore, Malaysia, which until more than two decades ago was riven with ethnic strife and a bleak economy, is now named as one of the most auspicious economies of the world.

Malaysia's prominent car, Proton, . . . agreed to be sold to Iran based on the trade deals ratified between the two countries. Turkey, which is still desperately struggling with its battered economy, has started to give signs of improvement when the plans for the total amount of exports has, [in 2003], exceeded 40 dollars (almost twice as much as that of Iran). Despite $170 billions of debt, if Turkey's endeavours of being admitted into the European Union reach fruition, nothing can preclude this country from improving the grim conditions inside.[1] These developments in the countries mentioned have taken place while Iran's economy has been facing horrendous problems caused by the mullahs' ill-advised economical policies, which have caused the life standard of an average Iranian from being higher than that of South Korea to fall as much as to the level of that of an average Algerian. . . .

Iran's Biggest Crisis

Twenty-four years from the revolution, the mullahs have miserably failed to create this so-called idyllic society they were so emphatically referring to. Instead, Iran is in the throes of the biggest political, social, and economical crisis of its recent history.

1. As of February 2006, Turkey had not been admitted.

Periodical Bibliography

The following articles have been selected to supplement the diverse views presented in this chapter.

Kaveh Basmenji   "Childhood's End," OpenDemocracy.net, June 17, 2005. www.opendemocracy.net

Jared A. Cohen and Abbas Milani   "The Passive Revolution," *Hoover Digest*, Fall 2005.

Nazila Fathi   "Iran: The Next Revolution?" *New York Times Upfront*, January 10, 2003.

Thomas L. Friedman   "Iran's Third Wave," *New York Times*, June 16, 2002.

Angus McDowall   "The New Populism," *Middle East Economic Digest*, July 1, 2005.

Afshin Molavi   "Our Allies in Iran," *New York Times*, November 3, 2005.

Afshin Molavi   "Tehran Dispatch: Fine China," *New Republic*, September 8, 2003.

Richard Seymour   "It's Not Over Yet," *Middle East*, April 2004.

Ray Takeyh and Nikolas K. Gvosdev   "Radical Islam: The Death of an Ideology?" *Middle East Policy*, Winter 2004.

For Further Discussion

Chapter 1

1. The authors in this chapter debate whether Iran is a threat to other nations, in particular the United States and Israel. If you believe that Iran is a threat to the latter, which of the two countries do you believe is at greater risk? If you do not believe that Iran is a threat, do you also agree with Edward S. Herman's argument that Iran is simply practicing self-defense should it choose to develop nuclear weapons? Explain your answers.

2. Douglas Davis asserts that Iran's plan is to use nuclear weapons to establish Islamic dominance across the globe. Based on your reading of his viewpoint and the others in this chapter, do you think such an outcome is possible? Why or why not?

3. A. William Samii argues that, due in large part to Iranian state radio, anti-American sentiment has grown in Iran. Do you think that the U.S. government should use radio to encourage pro-American feelings in Iran? Why or why not?

Chapter 2

1. Amnesty International and Paimaneh Hastaei disagree over the state of human rights in Iran. Who do you believe makes a more convincing argument and why?

2. In his viewpoint Farouz Farzami notes that Iranian reporters who censor themselves have been criticized by other journalists. If you were a journalist in a nation where the government controls public speech, how would you respond?

3. Four of the viewpoints in this chapter are by Iranians. Do you believe that the perspectives they offer are more valid than those of non-Iranians, or do you think that they are less likely to provide impartial views? Explain your answer.

Chapter 3

1. Having read the viewpoints in this chapter, do you believe that the United States should become more involved or less involved in Iran? Explain your answer, citing from the viewpoints.

2. Authors in the first chapter debated whether Iran is a nuclear threat, while the authors in this chapter consider how best to stem such a threat. Assuming such a threat exists, which solution do you think would be more effective: a military strike or diplomacy? Explain your answer, drawing from the viewpoints.

3. Geneive Abdo argues that the United States should not become involved in Iranian politics because previous efforts have failed. Do you think governments should base their foreign policy decisions on past history? Why or why not?

Chapter 4

1. After reading the viewpoints in this chapter, which issues do you think will have the greatest impact on Iran in the future? Explain.

2. Golnar Motevalli and Azadeh Moaveni disagree on the role that Iranian youth will play in bringing about political and social reform. Whose perspective do you find more convincing and why?

3. Reza Pahlavi is the son of the last shah of Iran, and thus the man who would have become ruler of Iran had the Islamic Revolution of 1979 not occurred. How does his background affect your response to his argument? Explain your answer.

Organizations to Contact

American Iranian Council (AIC)
20 Nassau St., Suite 111, Princeton, NJ   08542
(609) 252-9099 • fax: (609) 252-9698
e-mail: aic@american-iranian.org
Web site: www.american-iranian.org

The American Iranian Council is a nonprofit educational organization that aims to improve the relationship between the United States and Iran. The AIC also educates Americans about U.S.-Iran relations and serves as a forum for discussions of important Iranian issues. Publications available from AIC include the quarterly *AIC Insight*, several books, and an electronic bulletin, *AIC Update*.

Amnesty International (AI)
1 Easton St., London   WC1X 0DW
  UK
+44-20-74135500 • fax: +44-20-79561157
Web site: www.amnesty.org

Amnesty International is an international organization that seeks to end physical abuse, discrimination, censorship, and other human rights violations worldwide. AI publishes an annual report that details the condition of human rights around the world. Its Web site also includes reports and news about Iran.

Council on Foreign Relations (CFR)
58 E. Sixty-eighth St., New York, NY   10021
(212) 434-9400 • fax: (212) 434-9800
Web site: www.cfr.org

The CFR is a nonpartisan organization that holds meetings where world leaders, academics, government officials, and foreign-policy specialists debate world affairs. The council also supports a think tank where research is conducted on a variety of international issues. The council publishes reports, books, and the journal *Foreign Affairs*. Publications relating to Iran include *The Iran Nuclear Crisis* and *Iran's Nuclear Program: New Developments*.

Foundation for Iranian Studies

4343 Montgomery Ave., Bethesda, MD   20814
(301) 657-1990 • fax: (301) 657-1983
e-mail: fis@fis-iran.org
Web site: www.fis-iran.org

The Foundation for Iranian Studies is an educational and research institution that serves as a center for the study of Iranian history, cultural heritage, and contemporary political issues. It publishes the quarterly journal *Nameh*, which is published in Persian with article summaries in English. Its Web site includes an online photo gallery.

Human Rights Watch (HRW)

350 Fifth Ave., 34th Floor, New York, NY   10118-3299
(212) 290-4700 • fax: (212) 736-1300
e-mail: hrwnyc@hrw.org
Web site: www.hrw.org

Human Rights Watch is the largest U.S.–based human rights organization. Its researchers investigate human rights abuses throughout the world and publish their findings in books and reports, including *World Report 2006*, which includes a section on Iran. Other news about Iran and human rights, including issues such as censorship and the death penalty, is available on HRW's Web site.

International Atomic Energy Agency (IAEA)

PO Box 100, Wagramer Strasse 5, Vienna   A-1400
   Austria
(+431) 2600-0 • Fax: (+431) 2600-7
e-mail: official.mail@iaea.org
Web site: www.iaea.org

The IAEA is a worldwide organization that sets and promotes the application of standards for protecting people and the environment from the dangerous effects of nuclear radiation. It also works to promote safe and peaceful nuclear technologies. IAEA issues scientific and technical publications, the twice-yearly magazine *IAEA Bulletin*, annual reports, booklets, and fact sheets. News on Iran and nuclear weapons is also available on its Web site.

Iranian Women Studies Foundation (IWSF)
PO Box 380882, Cambridge, MA   02238-0882
(617) 492-9001 • fax: (617) 492-0111
e-mail: iranianwsf@aol.com
Web site: www.iwsf.org

IWSF is an organization that serves as a forum for the exchange of views on issues relating to Iranian women. It also disseminates information on the achievement of Iranian women and holds annual international conferences. Its Web site includes links to other organizations that are about women in Iran.

Middle East Media Research Institute (MEMRI)
PO Box 27837, Washington, DC   20038-7837
(202) 955-9070 • fax: (202) 955-9077
e-mail: memri@memri.org
Web site: www.memri.org

MEMRI is a nonpartisan organization that provides translations of Middle Eastern media and offers analysis of political, cultural, and religious trends in the area. Publications available on the Web site include the reports "The 'Second Islamic Revolution' in Iran: Power Struggle at the Top" and "Anti-semitism and Holocaust Denial in the Iranian Media."

National Iranian American Council (NIAC)
c/o OAI, 2801 M St. NW, Washington, DC   20007
(202) 719-8071 • fax: (202) 719-8097

e-mail: info@niacouncil.org
Web site: www.niacouncil.org

The objectives of the NIAC include helping Iranian-Americans foster greater understanding between the United States and Iran and building a network of Iranian-American organizations. NIAC projects include the Washington Policy Watch program, which helps the Iranian-American community respond to policy that affects them, and the Discrimination Center, which provides information on issues such as hate crimes and discrimination against immigrants.

Student Movement Coordination Committee for Democracy in Iran (SMCCDI)
5015 Addison Cir., #244, Addison, TX   75001
(972) 504-6864 • fax: (972) 491-9866
e-mail: smccdi@daneshjoo.org
Web site: http://www.daneshjoo.org/

The SMCCDI is an organization consisting of students both inside and outside Iran, along with Iranian professionals, who support the goal of a secular and democratic Iran. The organization also promotes human rights and free markets in Iran. Archived audio interviews and news about Iran are posted on its Web site.

Web sites

Reza Pahlavi's Secretariat
www.rezapahlavi.org

This is the Web site of Reza Pahlavi, the son of Mohammed Reza Pahlavi, the late shah of Iran. The site includes Pahlavi's speeches and interviews and news about Iran.

Women in Iran
www.womeniniran.net/english/

This Web site provides information on the issues and challenges facing Iranian women. It includes news, reports, and personal accounts written by women.

World Factbook: Iran

www.cia.gov/cia/publications/factbook/geos/ir.htm

This site is published by the Central Intelligence Agency. It provides a wide range of information on Iran, including its demographics, political structure, and economy.

Bibliography of Books

Geneive Abdo and Jonathan Lyons
Answering Only to God: Faith and Freedom in Twenty-First Century Iran. New York: Henry Holt, 2003.

Nafsin Alavi, ed. and trans.
We Are Iran. Brooklyn, NY: Soft Skull Press, 2005.

William O. Beeman
The "Great Satan" vs. the "Mad Mullahs": How the United States and Iran Demonize Each Other. Westport, CT: Praeger, 2005.

Ilan Berman
Tehran Rising: Iran's Challenge to the United States. Lanham, MD: Rowman & Littlefield, 2005.

Shahram Chubin
Whither Iran? Reform, Domestic Politics and National Security. Oxford, UK: Oxford University Press for the International Institute of Strategic Studies, 2002.

Anthony H. Cordesman
Iran's Developing Military Capabilities. Washington, DC: CSIS Press, 2005.

Jerome R. Corsi
Atomic Iran: How the Terrorist Regime Bought the Bomb and American Politicians. Nashville, TN: WND Books, 2005.

Bruce Cumings, Ervand Abrahamian, and Moshe Ma'oz
Inventing the Axis of Evil: The Truth About North Korea, Iran, and Syria. New York: New Press, 2004.

David R. Farber — *Taken Hostage: The Iran Hostage Crisis and America's First Encounter with Radical Islam*. Princeton, NJ: Princeton University Press, 2005.

David Harris — *The Crisis: The President, the Prophet, and the Shah; 1979 and the Coming of Militant Islam*. New York: Little, Brown, 2004.

Dilip Hiro — *The Iranian Labyrinth: Journeys Through Theocratic Iran and Its Furies*. New York: Nation Books, 2005.

Eric Hooglund, ed. — *Twenty Years of Islamic Revolution: Political and Social Transition in Iran Since 1979*. Syracuse, NY: Syracuse University Press, 2002.

Jane Mary Howard — *Inside Iran: Women's Lives*. Washington, DC: Mage Publishers, 2002.

Roger Howard — *Iran in Crisis? Nuclear Ambitions and the American Response*. London: Zed, 2004.

Christin Marschall — *Iran's Persian Gulf Policy: From Khomeini to Khatami*. London: RoutledgeCurzon, 2003.

Azadeh Moaveni — *Lipstick Jihad: A Memoir of Growing Up Iranian in America and American in Iran*. New York: Public Affairs, 2005.

Ali Mohammadi, ed. — *Iran Encountering Globalization: Problems and Prospects*. New York: RoutledgeCurzon, 2003.

Afshin Molavi   *Persian Pilgrimages: Journeys Across Iran*. New York: Norton, 2002.

Azar Nafisi   *Reading "Lolita" in Tehran*. New York: Random House, 2003.

Reza Pahlavi   *Winds of Change: The Future of Democracy in Iran*. Washington, DC: Regnery, 2002.

Kenneth M. Pollack   *The Persian Puzzle: The Conflict Between Iran and America*. New York: Random House, 2004.

Lloyd Ridgeon, ed.   *Religion and Politics in Modern Iran: A Reader*. London: Tauris, 2005.

Hammed Shahidian   *Women in Iran: Gender Politics in the Islamic Republic*. Westport, CT: Greenwood, 2002.

Behzad Yaghmaian   *Social Change in Iran: An Eyewitness Account of Dissent, Defiance, and New Movements for Rights*. Albany: State University of New York Press, 2002.

Index

European Union, 188
diplomatic efforts of, 21, 25–27, 108, 109–10, 119–28
human rights concerns of, 58, 59–60, 72
Iranian relations with, 16, 18, 114, 133, 143, 152
EU-3, 109–10, 127
see also Britain; France; Germany
exchange rates, 151
executions, 58, 65–66
of homosexuals, 96, 97
see also death penalty, use of
exports, 152, 187, 188
expression, freedom of. *See* speech, freedom of

family law, 75, 81–82, 88, 177
family planning, 148
Farsi, 15
Farzami, Farouz, 91
feminist movement, 75, 80–81
flogging, 66, 79, 86, 88, 89, 99–100
foreign exchange, 151, 152
Foundation for Iranian Studies, 193
Foundations of the Oppressed, 182
see also bonyads
France, 25, 109, 120, 127
freedoms, increasing, 157, 161, 163–64, 167, 169–70, 180

Gaddafi, Muammar, 22
Ganji, Akbar, 125
Germany, 15, 89–90
diplomatic efforts of, 25, 109, 110, 120, 127
Ghazi, Fereshteh, 88
government, 56, 58, 103, 129–40, 143–61, 177

see also clergy, government by; parliament
gozinesh, 60–61
Guardians' Council
candidates disqualified by, 60–61, 65, 130–31, 161
vetoes by, 78–79, 153
Guatemala, U.S. involvement in, 29–30, 35

Hamas, 40
hard-liners, 103, 139
economic reforms and, 147, 150–51, 159–61, 183–84
political reforms and, 78, 137, 143–44, 153, 178
Hastaei, Paimaneh, 67
health services, 70
Herman, Edward S., 28
Hezbollah, 32, 36, 38–39, 42, 46–47, 59, 107–8, 117
Higgins, William "Rich," 108
High Commission for Human Rights (UNHCHR), 73
hijab, 84
history, 14–16
homosexuals, discrimination against, 96–100
honor killings, 79
hostage crisis (1979-1980), 103, 116
see also revolutions, 1979
human rights, 56–101, 150, 180, 192
see also Iran, human rights violated by
Human Rights Dialogue, 59–60
Human Rights Watch (HRW), 193

incentives, economic, 25, 26, 120, 125, 127
income, per capita, 147–48
see also oil, income from